More Praise for
Stefanie Wilder-Taylor

"A former stand-up comic . . . and scabrously funny . . . Ms. Wilder-Taylor is built of nothing if not scrappiness, humor, luck, and demons."

—*The New York Times*

Praise for *It's Not Me, It's You*

"Her writing is rich with insights . . . So winning."

—*Entertainment Weekly*

Praise for *Naptime Is the New Happy Hour*

"Hilarious from cover to cover . . . She has a knack for both winding up in good stories and telling them."

—MamaPop.com

Praise for *Sippy Cups Are Not for Chardonnay*

"This book is hilarious. It's so real and funny. . . . I love it! I've read a lot of baby books, but I've never read anything like this before."

—Molly Shannon

"The kind of snarky straight talk you'd get from your best girlfriend."

—UrbanBaby.com

"Stefanie Wilder-Taylor offers a funny look at new motherhood . . . If you want to get inside a new mom's neurosis . . . this book is for you."

—*Chicago Tribune*

"Her sharp wit takes center stage . . . This little volume is perfect for spreading some joy on Mother's Day."

—*BookPage*

Also by Stefanie Wilder-Taylor

It's Not Me, It's You

Naptime Is the New Happy Hour

Sippy Cups Are Not for Chardonnay

I'm Kind of a Big Deal

and Other Delusions of Adequacy

STEFANIE WILDER-TAYLOR

Gallery Books

New York London Toronto Sydney

Gallery Books
A Division of Simon & Schuster, Inc.
1230 Avenue of the Americas
New York, NY 10020

First Gallery Books trade paperback edition June 2011

GALLERY BOOKS and colophon are trademarks of Simon & Schuster, Inc.

For information about special discounts for bulk purchases,
please contact Simon & Schuster Special Sales at 1-866-506-1949
or business@simonandschuster.com.

The Simon & Schuster Speakers Bureau can bring authors to
your live event. For more information or to book an event contact the
Simon & Schuster Speakers Bureau at 1-866-248-3049 or visit
our website at www.simonspeakers.com.

Manufactured in the United States of America

10   9   8   7   6   5   4   3   2   1

Library of Congress Cataloging-in-Publication Data

Wilder-Taylor, Stefanie.
  I'm kind of a big deal : and other delusions of adequacy / Stefanie Wilder-
Taylor.
     p. cm.
  1. Wilder-Taylor, Stefanie. 2. Women—United States—Biography.
3. Women comedians—United States—Biography. 4. Television writers—
United States—Biography. 5. Wilder-Taylor, Stefanie—Humor.
6. Interpersonal relations—Humor. 7. American wit and humor. I. Title.
  CT275.W558614A3 2011
  792.702'8092—dc22
  [B]   2010035943

ISBN 978-1-4391-7657-3
ISBN 978-1-4391-7697-9 (ebook)

For Putty

Contents

I'm Kind of
a Big Deal

The Sweaty Calzone

The summer I graduated high school, a few major things happened: Rebbie Jackson scored a Top 100 hit with "Centipede," catapulting her into the kind of Jackson-sibling fame previously experienced only by Marlon and Tito; I finally got through level three in Donkey Kong; and I ran away from home to become an actress in New York City. Actually I didn't intend to run away, and I don't know if it's really running away if no one actually notices you're gone—oh, and if you're almost *eighteen and out of high school*—but let's not split hairs; in my mind, I ran away.

I'd been living in Springfield, Massachusetts—home to the Basketball Hall of Fame, which I guess is impressive to people who aren't me—for the last two years of high school. In the couple months since I graduated (which was a miracle in itself), I'd been in a holding pattern. My days were spent waiting tables at a Bob's Big Boy franchise, where it wasn't unusual to receive tips of dimes and nickels for a party of five, and my nights were spent in my attic bedroom, where I occasionally entertained random boys with an intoxicating combination of smuggled Kahlúa, the pleasure of my company, and my Bonnie Tyler records. But I had bigger dreams: dreams of working at a more expensive restaurant with non-vinyl tablecloths; dreams of working in a classy establishment somewhere warm like California; dreams that just maybe that pricey bistro would have patio service. That was the thing about me: I dared to dream.

"You need to find somewhere to stay for ten days because we're going out of town on Friday," my mother announced when I came down for coffee one morning—and by morning I mean quarter of one.

"Why can't I just stay here?" I asked. I had no idea where I would go since I didn't exactly have any friends with their own apartments or even their own cars at this point.

"You haven't earned our trust, and I don't feel I can leave you in this house while we're gone." My mother wasn't a stranger to asking other peoples' parents to watch me while she and my stepfather went out of town, expecting them to provide me with a bed, discipline, rides to and from school, and plenty of snacks. But that was the seventies and this was the eighties, times had changed and people took a slightly harsher view of freeloading. And of course now she was making me do the asking, which was even worse.

Clearly, I was left with only one choice: pretend to have a place to go, then once they left town, come back and let myself into my own house with my own key. Me untrustworthy? That was laughable!

At the end of the week my parents left for their vacation and I made an elaborate show of leaving for a friend's house. "Good-bye! Have a wonderful trip! I'll just be at 'my friend's house'! The whole time! Until you get back!" Later that afternoon, I arrived back at my empty house with my suitcase, about 10 percent of my high school senior class, and a pony keg. But when I unlocked the door and started to push it open I was met with the immediate and unmistakable resistance of a bolt lock. My parents had bolted the door with an almost-never-used key that I didn't have. It was as if they *expected* me to try to sneak back into my own house. Well now, this was infuriating. And even if the assembled crowd didn't represent the A-list of my class, it was still pretty embarrassing.

I made my way around to the back of the house and tried a few other doors, hoping against hope that somehow in their zeal to bar me from my own house they'd neglected to lock a side door. No such luck; my parents were on their game. Not wanting to give up too easily, especially since I had an audience, I struggled to get up to the second floor and climb in through the bathroom window. Miraculously, it was unlocked. With one knee still on the windowsill and one leg back on the ladder I'd pulled out from the garage, I turned around to see my neighbors, Don and Sue Petofsky, eyeing me from their living room window just as I dropped out of sight and into the bathtub.

Once my friends were in the house, the mini keg was tapped and red plastic cups (the choice of un-derage drinkers nationwide) were quickly being filled when the knock came at the front door. My neighbors had reported me breaking into *my own house*. I prob-ably had it coming: for the last three years I'd walked around naked in my attic bedroom, which opened toward their master bedroom, and for two of those years my windows had no shades. Turns out Sue was a bit of a window-treatment Nazi or didn't appreciate me dancing in front of it to Bonnie Tyler. Either way, it was payback time.

I was told by the police that I had to vacate immediately, which is how I found myself on an Amtrak to move in with my friend Jackie and become a star of stage and screen in New York City.

Jackie was an acquaintance from high school in Washington State, where we'd lived before I moved to Massachusetts just prior to my junior year. We were both Jewish, and in northern Washington—a beer run from Hayden Lake, Idaho, which is practically the Aryan Nation headquarters—Jews were about as welcome as a black jellybean, so we tended to stick together. I think Jackie thought I was funny and it's also possible she'd never met someone whose mom sewed all her clothes. In all honesty, the thing that drew me to Jackie was the Visa card her father gave her in her own name. Growing up, credit cards among fellow teens were like a Sasquatch to me; I suspected their existence but seeing one made me want to whip out my camera so I could prove it. I felt the exact same way about appetizers. Jackie's father owned five or six See's Candies franchises and despite their sky-high dental bills, they were rolling in dough. I absolutely loved to hear Jackie say, "Charge it, please," and I'd ask her to repeat it over and over in foreign accents.

Occasionally we'd blow off school entirely to have lunch at the Spokane Club, where we could give Jackie's dad's credit card a serious workout. Our usual order was lobster bisque soup, shrimp cocktails, and iceberg lettuce salads with extra Roquefort dressing on the side plus around six Tab colas. The most dangerous thing about Tab seemed to be a medicinal aftertaste and a slightly elevated risk of bladder cancer. At fourteen this was of small concern to me, so I was a raging Tabaholic.

Eventually I moved to Massachusetts and Jackie's parents sent her to NYU to study theater. Looking back, other than our Tab habit and us both being Jews, Jackie and I had very little in common. So it quite possibly may have been a mistake to call her out of the blue and invite myself to stay.

I had just enough money to buy a one-way ticket to Grand Central Station. Given that Jackie and I had been very good friends for about six months in the tenth grade, I figured once I got there she'd be pretty thrilled that I had reentered her life, and I would have no need to ever come home. Plus, wasn't New York basically just LA with shittier weather? This was going to be great! A new life. Also, this would be quite the life lesson for my untrusting parents. They'd be sorry when I was a big star in New York and the only way that they could spend time with me would be to fight the throngs of fans outside of Radio City Music Hall (or wherever big shots of my caliber hung out) before I was whisked out of sight in my limo. Of course I would speak kindly of them to the press because I wouldn't hold a grudge. I would have learned that grudges serve no purpose on my spiritual path. Kaballah would have taught me that. So yes, there would have been much learning.

The trouble started when Jackie met me at the station. I spotted her right away dressed in all black, save for a purple wool fedora hat with a feather that extended a city block from the brim. It was truly horrifying. The only circumstance in which it's acceptable to wear a felt hat with a giant feather is if you're a cartoon pimp from 1974 or Pinocchio. Other than that, my official opinion is just no. Plus, if she was now the sort of person who would wear a huge feather in her hat, what other bad decisions was she making?

"I hope sharing my bed is okay," Jackie said as soon as she let me into her studio apartment. I'd made the mistake of assuming that all rich folks had bedrooms, if not entire wings of their homes, to spare. Clearly I had some learning to do about New York real estate. Needless to say, I was caught off guard by the intimacy of the setup.

"Yeah, why wouldn't it be?" Just because she lived in New York now and I lived in Springfield did not mean that I was uptight.

"Great. I'm so glad you're here. I think we're going to have an absolutely fabulous time together. What's it been? Two years? Feels like aaages," Jackie mewed at me in a decidedly affected tone of voice. I wasn't sure if she was channeling Mrs. Howell or a character from *Eloise*. I half expected her to call me daaahling and invite me to the Plaza. "African tea?" she asked, walking into the kitchen, and by kitchen I mean a hot plate on a windowsill that held a single cracked teacup.

"No, thanks. I'm more of a domestic gal. Do you have a Miller Lite?" I really felt the need to take the edge off and peered around her kitchenette.

"I never drink beer. Wasted calories." She laughed a laugh that could've been a sneeze. "I've put on a few pounds since I've been here," Jackie said while stripping off her clothes. "What do you think?" I was more concerned that she seemed to have gained about fourteen new personalities.

And there she was, standing in front of me stark

naked. And then I noticed the Grace Jones poster on the wall and I started to get really uncomfortable.

After a couple of days Jackie had a "Welcome, Stefanie" cocktail party with four or five female friends. Except there were no cocktails. She just served espresso, so it was actually more of a strong, bitter coffee party without men. There wouldn't have been any food either, except that one of Jackie's neighbors brought along a toaster oven from her apartment so we could heat croissants. But in order to use it, we had to unplug the espresso maker because the circuit couldn't handle both.

A woman in a tight T-shirt named Evelyn tried to engage me in a conversation about feminist film theory. Naturally, Evelyn wasn't wearing a bra. She had the kind of breasts that made up for in nipple what they lacked in cup size. I'm sure from her perspective she was braless to punctuate her feminist status, and it's possible that she burned her bras before her whole flapjack-nipple situation got so out of control, but the whole look was nauseating and made it impossible to have a conversation. Oh, also making it impossible to have a conversation? My lack of interest in feminist film theory.

I tried to break into another exchange between two women about sustainable artisan cheese shares. "Anyone been watching *Knots Landing*?" I interrupted, figuring that although I knew nothing about feminism or cheese, I was a savant when it came to prime-time soaps, and come on, that had to count for something.

"I've never heard of it," the one in army pants said.

"What?" How was that even possible?

"I don't really watch TV unless it's the news," the other one said in agreement.

"What do you mean? Not even *Dynasty*?" I couldn't keep the incredulousness out of my voice. Don't watch TV? And they called themselves theater students? Was I on *Candid Camera*? Well, obviously not, because it was doubtful any of these assholes had ever seen it.

I felt like I really needed to sit down and catch my breath. With seven women in two hundred square feet the air seemed sucked out of the room with a vacuum. Plus the four shots of espresso I'd downed in desperation were making me edgy, irritable, and not a little bit dizzy. These were not my kind of people and I was beginning to despise them.

I sat next to Jackie on the bed, which, besides a few folding chairs that were taken, was the only place to sit. "What I got out of this article is the idea that Kafka's humor revolves around making abstract notions concrete," she was saying to her friend in a crocheted dress. I closed my eyes, hoping to leave my body for the remainder of the evening. That's when Jackie started giving me a neck massage.

I was definitely not living the dream, that much was clear. What I wanted to do was hightail it to Grand Central Station and hop the next Amtrak back home, but I had no money. If I wanted to unrun away, I was going to have to get money, and that meant getting a job immediately . . . and getting a job immediately left me with few options since my only real useful skill was carrying seventeen plastic glasses of water without the use of a tray.

Here I'd thought I could laze around for a few weeks enjoying the city before buying a pair of leg warmers and hitting the streets for all the major casting calls. I'd seen *Fame* and I realized that the life of a struggling actor was going to be difficult. But I didn't think that most struggling actors were forced to lay stock still in their friend's bed all night *acting* like they were fast asleep, all the while hoping against hope that they didn't wake up and find they'd become an accidental lesbian.

I'm not stupid; I knew that there would be dues

to be paid. Look, Coco did some things she regretted, and I'm sure she was just doing what she needed to do to make it in the biz. But this just seemed too high a price to pay. Maybe I just didn't want it bad enough. Maybe I didn't have what it takes to make it in the big city. Or possibly it just wasn't my time.

Thank God this was New York City and there were approximately eighty-five restaurants per square mile. What I lacked in restaurant experience the Big Apple food service industry made up for in demand. I threw on a short skirt and got hired at the first place I walked into, a midpriced Italian restaurant called Il Calzone di Canto (which the busboys told me loosely translated to "The Sweating Calzone"), in spite of the fact that the only experience I had serving Italian food was the spaghetti and meatballs from the kids' menu at Bob's Big Boy. The only *minor* hitch in my plan was that it was a singing job. After serving up a big plate of piping-hot lasagna or whatever, apparently I was going to have to belt out "O Sole Mio." I assured the manager I had a professional singing voice and was surprised and a little horrified that he took my word for it. Sooner or later I'd have to sing for someone's supper.

Years later I would come across a similar dilemma when I seriously contemplated a stint as a stripper. A woman I met at a bar tried to talk me and a friend into joining her in stripping in Vegas on the weekends. I wasn't totally against the plan after hearing that I could easily make a few grand in a night, but I did feel there were a couple of roadblocks. "Let me just lay this out on the table: I have quite a bit of cellulite," I told the girl.

"Oh my God. That is not a problem at *all*," she said reassuringly. "First off you can wear a little scarf over your ass if you really feel self-conscious, and it's pretty dark, so don't even worry about it." I felt my cellulite situation would require more than a little scarf and some dim lighting but I tried to keep an open mind. "Actually some men love big butts. The booty boys, we call them." I practically gagged on my beer but tried not to show it.

"Okay, well, my only other real issue is the dancing part. I don't have a lot of rhythm and I've never done any sort of pole work."

"You've danced in a dance club. It's the same thing. The real money is in the lap dances, but all the girls are supposed to take at least one turn dancing onstage. All you have to do is avoid it for a couple of shifts. Look, when you see the kind of money you can make, you'll get over all your hesitation." The more we talked and the more I drank the more doable it sounded that night. Then I woke up the next morning sober and realized I was simply too prudish to go through with it.

Right now I needed cash, and I wasn't going to let a lack of vocal talent stand in the way of getting out of New York and out of Jackie's pansexual studio apartment. She was in school when I left for my first training shift at Il Calzone di Canto, but I could tell she'd been there recently from the stench of imported tea and because she'd left a cassette tape of the soundtrack to *42nd Street* playing on the stereo. I practically broke the stop button trying to turn it off. I really wasn't looking forward to spending another night in Jackie's bed smelling her natural body odor. One other new affectation of the big city seemed to be her holistic deodorizing crystal, which she used in place of deodorant. It may have given her healing energy or whatever crystals are supposed to do, but killing odor was not within its mystical powers.

My first night at Il Calzone di Canto went well since it was my job mainly to just watch and carry plates of shrimp scampi and veal parmigiana behind Bert, the pasta-slinging baritone I'd been assigned to shadow. About halfway through the night all the servers gathered on a riser next to Rocco the piano player and performed their hearts out. Honestly, you'd have thought they were waiting on the casting director from *Cats* by the way they were busting out the vibrato. Yet another thing I didn't like about New York: everyone was obsessed with Broadway.

Two nights later, I was allowed three tables to wait on throughout the night, which finally allowed me to make tips that wouldn't immediately have to be handed over to Bert. I'd managed to pull in about seventy dollars before hearing piano man Rocco boom out, "Now let's welcome up our newest addition to the *famiglia*!" And just like that, the jig was up. There was no way this could be anything but humiliating. Rocco dragged out *"famigliaaaaaa"* just long enough for me to ponder if I could get someone to murder him really quick, but I had a sneaking suspicion most people in that line of work would be childhood friends of Rocco anyhow. I walked toward the stage, feeling like I was headed to the gallows. I could hear one of my tables calling to me from what seemed like a million miles away, "Miss, I need a sambuca." *So do I, my friend, so do I.*

"What do you want to sing, doll?" Rocco asked.

"It doesn't matter," I answered truthfully, resigned to my fate. So he played the opening bars to "That's Amore" and I did my best to sing it, but I knew I was done.

On the Amtrak back to Springfield, eating a whole bag of garlic knots I'd stolen from the Sweaty Calzone on my way out the door, I knew I'd made the right decision. I was clearly not a New Yorker. New Yorkers were way too focused on the theater. Most of the actors there took themselves way too seriously, arriving at auditions with ten years of dance and vocal training. I had a feeling that my acting was going to be better suited for a place like Los Angeles where they made TV. Television would require a lot less singing and dancing, and more importantly, less training. It seemed to me that all you needed to arrive with in LA was your vibe.

I braced myself for trouble as I walked up to my front door, but the door caught as I went to push it open. It was still bolted because my parents weren't back yet. After all, it had been only a week. Seeing no car in Don and Sue's neighboring driveway, I climbed the ladder and let myself back into my house. I grabbed a handful of pretzels from the pantry and called Jackie. "I'm so sorry I left without warning," I said, "but thanks to your generous hospitality you helped me realize that I've always wanted to open my own feminist bookshop–slash–bead store and . . . well . . . a great space opened up in Northampton, so I had to rush back." And with that, I quickly got off the phone, because *Highway to Heaven* was starting and DVRs had yet to be invented.

I Blame Bob Dylan

Remember when a pre-*Friends* Courteney Cox was invited onstage in that 1984 Bruce Springsteen video for "Dancing in the Dark" and later became a huge star? Well, a very similar thing happened to me in 1985 when I was plucked from obscurity to be featured in a Bob Dylan music video! And then dropped back into obscurity twelve hours later.

"They're filming some video at the church on Franklin and Highland where my Tuesday AA meeting's at and they need female extras. You guys should go do it," my friend Tanya's alcoholic aunt announced, just before taking a drag of her cigarette and blowing out a smoke ring. She was one of those alcoholics who wanted to have her cake and drink it too: she went to meetings but still proudly drank like a fish. Much later I would find out something she already knew: AA meetings are excellent networking opportunities.

My high school BFF, Beth, and I had just pulled into Hollywood in my yellow Mazda GLC that day after a two-week road trip from Springfield, Massachusetts. Our worldly possessions now included only what would fit into the hatchback of the aging subcompact. We had clothes, makeup, and a cooler of groceries, which contained the large box of Slim Jims and some candy we'd stolen from the lobby of a Flagstaff, Arizona, Motel 6 when a forty-minute wait and numerous clangs on the night bell resulted in neither the night manager nor a room. Tired, hungry, and surly from twelve un-air-conditioned hours on the interstate, we decided the motel at least owed us a delicious processed meat treat for our trouble.

Tanya's aunt had hesitantly agreed to put us up for a few days while we looked for jobs and an apartment, and at first she hardly seemed to be the model of hospitality. But suddenly here she was, giving us our first big break in the biz. I made a mental note to thank her in a future acceptance speech.

"What's the video? Do you know?" I hoped it was the Go-Go's, because they were my favorite band, and I'd been trying to figure out a way for quite a while to let them know that their video for "Vacation" had almost inspired me to learn to water-ski.

"It's a Bob Dylan, Dave Stewart song," she answered.

"Dave Stewart?"

"Isn't he one half of the Eurythmics?"

"Huh." That sounded fairly big-time.

Beth and I didn't have a huge game plan. We were done with our old lives and ready for fame and fortune—all we needed was an entrée. This was perfect. We'd just nodded to Mr. T at a self-serve Exxon the day before, so we already had our feet wet when it came to hanging with celebrities.

Knowing that the Springsteen chick (we wouldn't know her name was Courteney until she turned up four years later in the waning days of *Family Ties,* when suddenly Alex Keaton was having sex with "that chick from the Springsteen video") had become the 1984 music video "it" girl by appearing in the "Dancing in the Dark" video, I figured all I had to do was get a solo dance in this video and the rest would be history. Truth be told, I wasn't a major Dylan fan—I was half a generation too young to really remember when he was in his prime—but he didn't need to know that. Plus, I couldn't imagine that Court had been that into

Bruce Springsteen. The guy always looks like he's just mowed every lawn in the neighborhood and then realized there's no time for a shower before hitting the stage. I don't relate to Dylan songs, mostly because they sound too much like he's singing them while underneath an old Dodge doing a brake job. It's just all muffled mumbly jumbly. I don't get it, but then again I once downloaded a Taylor Hicks song from iTunes, so my taste in music isn't to be trusted.

After getting dressed up in all the Chess King–style clothes we owned (think Wet Seal with half the Lycra and twice the zippers), the three of us crowded into Tanya's aunt's small bathroom and applied all the eyeliner we owned to our top lids and the inside of our bottom lids in an attempt to look sultry and sophisticated. We split a can of Aqua Net and then crammed on as many O-rings (jelly bracelets?) as would fit on our arms and slid on our ripped lace gloves. I then doused myself in body glitter and, as a distinguished finishing touch, applied a fake beauty mark with a dark brown eyebrow pencil halfway between my nose and my lips. For me, eight days at U Mass Amherst had shown me that higher education was not to be my avenue to success. But a Bob Dylan cameo? This was my up elevator! And if it could happen for that Springsteen

chick, it could damn well happen for me. Just for luck
I drained a few more sprays out of the dying Aqua Net
can before heading out.

It wasn't difficult to find parking at the church in
the heart of Hollywood. Almost the entire block right
in front of the entrance was completely clear. This was
a good omen since I'd heard a lot of rumors that the
most difficult things to find in LA were parking and
good pizza. So far, wrong on both counts. I'd already
had a delicious piece of pizza at a newish place called
Domino's and now I'd found the perfect parking space.
Things were already going far better than I'd expected.

The scene inside the church auditorium was cha-
otic. Tanya, Beth, and I looked for someone who appeared to be in charge, but no one seemed to have any
idea what was going on. At least a hundred and fifty
people were crammed into a fairly small space. Sweaty
kids in half shirts leaned against the makeshift stage
while roadies set up monster amps and speakers.

"Thanks for dressing up, guys," I said under my
breath to Beth. Having lived in New York City for a
week I'd gotten used to a certain level of professional-
ism, and this wasn't cutting it. After about an hour
of wandering aimlessly around the place waiting for
something to happen, I was feeling a lot less enthused

about the whole thing. We'd hadn't had a single Dylan sighting and we didn't know if we'd seen Dave Stewart since none of us had a clue what he looked like.

"What do you think we should do?" Beth asked me.

"How the hell should I know?" I shot back. Beth had a habit of thinking I knew all the answers. I'd just turned nineteen to her seventeen, so I did understand that she looked up to me in a way. But the reality was I felt just as lost as she did, I was just more practiced in my false bravado.

"Do you think we should go home?" she asked, lighting a Kool menthol. Not wanting to be responsible for someone else's fate when I could barely take charge of my own, I nervously snapped, "Let's give it a few more minutes," and sat down on a folding chair. It was times like these that I was pissed I'd never taken up smoking. There was a brief period in high school when I'd put in a solid effort to develop a cigarette habit just to fit in. The problem was I couldn't actually inhale without feeling like my lungs were catching fire, so I'd taken to carrying around the same pack of Marlboro Reds for about three months, occasionally pretending to smoke one. Finally, to my vascular relief, I met a new circle of friends who were mostly focused on drinking.

Another hour went by before a rocker chick with

a microphone walked up on the stage and addressed the crowd. "Hi, everyone," she yelled, creating monster feedback. "We're ready to start the shoot!" There were about two halfhearted whoops from the crowd, which is the moment I realized that the majority of these people weren't even there for the video. On closer investigation, most of them were just hanging out in the hopes that some free weed might trickle down. And *that's* when I got even more excited about my chances of being a star.

Soon Bob Dylan and Dave Stewart were onstage playing guitar over a prerecorded version of their song "When the Night Comes Falling from the Sky." The crowd was instructed to dance and generally look like we were being escorted by angels to the highest level of hard-rock heaven. We did as instructed, take after take, for four exhausting hours. When Bob and Dave took breaks Rock Chick came out to make sure we stayed where we were "for continuity."

"You know what? This is ridiculous. I need to talk to my agent about what's going on around here."

"You don't have an agent," Beth said. "In fact, you don't even know an agent."

"Well, someone from my team," I said, digging around for my Hershey's Kiss lip gloss, which I'd been reapplying every twenty seconds. It was dry in the church despite all the sweaty bodies, and I hadn't had anything to drink in over four hours. I hoped this wasn't indicative of what was in store for the rest of my video-vixen career. I wasn't expecting beluga caviar but a Diet Coke would have been appreciated.

"I'm tired. Fuck this, I'm sooo ready to bail," Beth whined in my ear. She was seriously working my nerves now. I knew she was young, but she clearly had no idea what it took to make it in the industry. We were going to have to muster a lot more stamina. Hell, I was tired too, but there was no way we were leaving. The crowd had already thinned, increasing our opportunities for camera time.

"How's my mole?" I asked Tanya, who was dancing maniacally to my right. "Is it still intact or is it smudging off?"

"It might need a touch-up," she yelled over the chorus, which was playing for at least the 417th time. I feared I would never for as long as I lived be able to remove this song from my brain. I worried it had recorded over some valuable information, like my ability to swear in Spanish or twirl a baton. And I certainly didn't want to have to remove that from the "special skills" section of my résumé.

As Tanya danced, the roach-clip feathers she'd clipped in her hair whipped around and hit me in the face repeatedly, again endangering the mole, which was now my trademark in the video community. Another hour went by without a break and I had to admit it was getting tedious. I was already on the verge of collapse when things took a sudden turn for the worse. A skinny brunette with majestically feathered hair and big, professionally heavily made-up eyes came in through the back door flanked by roadies. A bunch of production staff walked around with her putting tape on the floor, mapping out her marks. I was horrified. There *was* a solo dance to be had, and it was already spoken for.

"This is so not cool. What does that girl have that we don't? Other than higher cheekbones and a shitload of tangerine blush?" Beth said. *And maybe twenty fewer pounds,* I couldn't help but think morosely. And while I was thinking about being possibly the fattest aspiring actress in Hollywood who wasn't aiming for roles like the mouthy best friend, I got a serious craving for one of those Slim Jims I knew was waiting in the back of my car. I felt I'd earned a few after all the hard-core dancing I'd done so far. I knew I had to replace the sodium I'd lost through all my sweating; any athlete would tell you the same thing. This was it. We needed to get out of there if we were to keep any of our dignity intact. I gestured to Tanya and Beth that I was ready to go, but as we angled toward the exit, Rocker Chick came running over.

"Oh, please, you guys," she yelled over chorus number ninety million, "we just need you a little longer." I could barely hear her, possibly from the onset of permanent inner ear damage resulting from four hours dancing next to eight-foot stack speakers. "UHM MUF GRMN FLAG. . . . We're going to feature you." That I heard.

Soon Tanya, Beth, and I were positioned near the stage, dancing our hearts out with renewed energy in our new "featured" role: leading a path for Tangerine Blush Girl to walk past and up toward the stage, where Bob Dylan was waiting for her. It was so romantic, and I was grateful to be such an integral part of their story. The three of us mouthed the words to the song we now knew by heart—at this point I was convinced I wrote it—and clapped along to the music for another two hours straight.

Finally back outside the church, we were surprised to see it was pitch-dark already before realizing it was almost midnight. My feet felt like they'd been run over by a herd of angry buffalo. I really could've used a Percocet, which I didn't have. I wondered how many videos I'd have to be a featured friend of the lead dancer in before my Screen Actors Guild health insurance kicked in. I'd need a good health care plan if I was going to have unnecessary dental surgery any time soon.

We trudged up the street a few yards looking for the telltale dirty yellow of my car. It was hard to miss, but we didn't see it. "I know we parked right here," I said, gesturing to the space now occupied by a different car in front of the church.

"Maybe it was a little farther up," Tanya said. It may have been twelve hours but I knew for a fact that we parked *right out front*. I wandered up the street a ways trying to make sense of not seeing my car where I left it. Was I hallucinating? My heart was starting to beat in my chest and my mind was racing. *Has my car been stolen? Who would steal a yellow Mazda with no a/c, only an AM/FM radio, and a broken cassette player? The only place they'd be driving would be straight to a mechanic. But* oh my God *someone stole my car. There is no other explanation.* I went from almost my highest high to my lowest low. Everything I owned was in that car. Being a responsible traveler, I'd had the money I'd saved for my trip converted into traveler's checks. But what was left of those traveler's checks was packed in the back of my car, probably joyriding their way around East Hollywood as I stood there dumbfounded.

"What do we do?" Beth asked, looking at me help-lessly.

"I don't know!" I yelled. *"I don't know everything!"* I'd really had it with people and their helplessness. I knew I was flying off the handle and that it wasn't her fault, but hey, people needed to cut me some slack. *I'm an artist now,* I thought, *we're known for our uneven temperament.* I felt so completely exhausted and de-feated in that moment. I couldn't even imagine what I would do without a car, money, food. I'd lived here for all of twenty-four hours, and LA had already kicked my ass. Suddenly I wanted my mom.

A town car pulled out of the church's driveway and came to a stop near where I stood crying. The window rolled down and I could make out a pair of shades. I rightfully assumed the only person who would be wearing shades at midnight was Bob Dylan.

"Are you girls all right?" he rasped. There were a lot more people in the car, but the important thing was Bob was the one addressing us.

"Someone stole my car," I said with a sniffle.

"Was it parked here?" he asked, peering over his sunglasses to assess the situation.

"Yes, right here!" Did Bob think I was just confused? Maybe he'd just never met anyone with such good parking karma before.

"This is a no-parking zone, hon." He gestured to the No Parking sign that was conveniently positioned about a foot away from where I was standing. "You must've been towed."

"Towed?" I couldn't stop the tears now. Beth and Tanya weren't nearly as broken up as I was because, screw it, it wasn't *their* car. Their possessions were safely locked in a tow yard. Suddenly, this was my problem.

"Why did you park here?" Beth whined. I could've punched her. But I didn't want to seem abusive in front of Bob. I knew just enough from my counterculture parents to know that he was all about peace, antiwar movements, showering with Joan Baez, and positive stuff like that. I wanted to prove to him that I could handle myself under adversity. Also I didn't want to get edited out of the video for violence.

"There's a phone number on the sign you can call to get your car back," Bob said. *How does Bob know all this?* I wondered. I couldn't imagine that he'd had to drive his own car in the last decade. Plus, he was a rocker, a rebel; what the hell did he care about no-parking zones?

"Thank you, Mr. Dylan," I said. "I'll just go and call then. Thanks. Really."

"Mr. Dylan, I just want to tell you I'm a huge fan! I have all of your albums!" Beth lied. I can't say I didn't respect her for it though. She was starting to show some of the qualities it would take to make it in this town.

"Me too," Tanya said.

"Thank you. And good luck, girls." With that, the window rolled up and the town car rolled on into the night.

The next day, after we'd retrieved my car with a little help from Beth's Bar Mitzvah fund, we decided we were all officially Bob Dylan fans. To celebrate we went out and bought *Blood on the Tracks,* one of Bob's most famous albums according to the assistant manager at Tower Records. We put it on and played it all the way through, and I have to admit, I kind of got it. I could see why people love Bob Dylan. I mean, "Tangled Up in Blue"? "Shelter from the Storm"? "You're Gonna Make Me Lonesome When You Go"? Wow, those were some good songs, and I could absolutely see why they'd have such an effect on his fans.

Unfortunately, "When the Night Comes Falling from the Sky" did not have any such effect on any of Dylan's old fans, nor did it create any new fans. The song peaked at number 33 on the U.S. *Billboard* charts and then fell off into oblivion. Let's put it this way: it was no "Dancing in the Dark." And thus, I never became Courteney Cox-Arquette. I never even had a chance. I did my part but Bob didn't do his, and although things worked out in the end, I have to admit, I'm still a little bitter.

The Flying Handelmans

"My trouble is, I'm named Bernard. Who made it my name? Did I make it my name? I don't feel like a Bernard. I had hostile parents, and they named me Bernard. Is that my fault?

"No. 'My trouble is,' *pause*, 'I'm named *Bernard*,'" my father said, correcting me. I was standing on a black stage in a small studio space in the Valley where my father taught acting and stand-up comedy classes, performing a monologue from something called *Feiffer's People* for the twentieth time. Either it was his favorite monologue that had ever been written by any playwright in the history of theater, or he was simply too lazy to dig up something from this decade. From what I knew of him, I couldn't help but suspect it was the latter.

My father, Stanley Myron Handelman, was a moderately famous television comedian in the late sixties and early seventies. During his brief heyday, he filled theaters, palled around with the Rat Pack, and appeared on all the major talk shows. He did *The Merv Griffin Show* over thirty times, more than any other comedian, he would've been happy to tell you without prompting. I'd recently been reunited with him after about eight years of living in different parts of the country with my mother and stepfather and having virtually no contact with him.

One of the first things he did was invite me to take his class. I knew he'd been teaching stand-up comedy and acting for years; in fact, I remembered quite clearly when I was about fourteen years old, on a visit to Los Angeles, sitting in an auditorium, watching him teach a class to a group of eager young students. He hadn't done a television appearance in years at that point, but his students seemed to really look up to him. He was a god to them—if God had trained for his heavenly duties in the Catskills, wearing a newsboy cap and dark-rimmed glasses. Like a lot of people, Stan's students were captivated by his charisma and charm. So captivated, in fact, one of those students married him and became wife number four, succeeding my mother, who had filled the role of number three. She was twenty-six years old to his fifty-four.

My mother had remarried very soon after the divorce, but my new stepfather was neither suited for nor remotely interested in the role of surrogate dad. So, from the age of four onward, instead of two dads, there was a paternal placeholder in my life. In true Psych 101 fashion, I had a driving need to prove myself worthy of the fatherly approval that was in short supply. Add in my issues with food and body image, and it was like I'd been assembled in a lab from pieces of other needy chicks to finance therapists' vacation homes and retirements.

After I moved to Los Angeles and tracked my father down at a local comedy/jazz club performing, we'd created a tenuous relationship based partially on my desire to forge a connection with the father I never really knew and partially on my fascination with the art of stand-up comedy—which, in hindsight, were probably one and the same. In addition to taking his class, I'd started going to a comedy club nestled in a San Fernando Valley Hilton on Sunday nights to watch some of his students who'd formed a comedy troupe. They were a group of approximately eight guys, coached by Stan and going by the name the Flying Handelmans. I got to see them work on new material they'd honed in class, tighten bits that were already working, and figure out why certain jokes that worked in class didn't work in front of a live audience. These guys seemed like pros onstage and were usually funny as hell. Although I wasn't sure if I had the talent, I wanted to be a part of them and gain membership into Stan's world, which to me would be the ultimate acceptance. But if I ever hoped to gain entrée to their performance group, I had to perform this crap-ass monologue. Again.

"My trouble is . . ." I waited and waited, letting the words marinate on my tongue, feeling the neurotic Jewish energy of the character take over my entire being, my essence, building up pressure that demanded release. "I'm named *Bernard.*" I dropped "Bernard" like a bomb. *Ka-boom!* I imagined the word bursting from my mouth and shattering the atmosphere, the molecular mass of air no match for the intensity, the very *spirit* I'd given to the word "Bernard."

"Eh, I don't believe you. I don't believe you're really Bernard. Do *you* believe it? Because if you're not feeling it, how are you going to make us believe it? I'm trying to help you. Do it again from the top." And here he rolled his hand in front of his chest in an upward motion as if he were showing me how to bring forth the force of these words. "My trouble is . . ."

"My trouble is, I'm named Bernard," I said again with far less gusto.

"No. It's still not believable," Stan said to me like I was the lowliest of his students, not there by invitation from him to take him up on his offer to be closer, to have a relationship, to share in the sole thing he could offer me. But as for the monologue, he was right. It wasn't believable.

"Maybe we could do a different monologue," I suggested casually, as if it hadn't been suggested by a hundred other students in a hundred other classes he'd taught over the years. *But I'm his daughter,* I thought to myself. *Maybe I can get through to him that this monologue is like a dinosaur all dressed up in a suit trying to live in people-land.*

"This is a really dynamite monologue, Stef. It doesn't matter what you perform, what the words are, it's the part of *you* that you put into your words. And that's a skill. Do your work with mastery." My father had become a Buddhist, perhaps as a genuine spiritual quest, or maybe because he was under the impression that Buddhists don't pay taxes. In any event, there was lots of free-flowing philosophy dropped on his students throughout the three hours we were together every week.

Today's lesson wasn't over yet. "That's what I'm trying to teach here; it's my life's work. I've performed on a lot of shows, I did *Merv Griffin* more times than any other comedian, and the reason I was booked, the reason, is my delivery. No one could deliver a joke like that. The words themselves are not the most important ingredient. You are the most important ingredient." We all made ourselves comfortable because Stan was getting on a roll. "The way you build your stand-up act is by being a great actor; you draw the audience in with the same sleight of hand as that of a magician, lulling them into the next zany joke or story. You need to become animated, using your voice, facial expressions, and body language to fascinate and mystify the audience. So I want all of you to do it again."

One by one, we'd all perform the first few lines of the monologue, and one by one, two black guys, a couple of white women, and a short Italian Catholic took on Bernard, trying to reach the deeper meaning, the existential truth of a dude with an unfortunate moniker.

"Sorry if I was a little hard on you today in class, Stef," he said once we were the only people left in the studio. I'd outlasted the couple of students who'd hung out after to try out a quick joke or pick my father's brain about their act. As he talked he packed his monologue sheets and other papers into the black satchel he always carried with him. "I can't treat you differently than the rest of the students or they might feel it's unfair." I understood that, and I actually hadn't expected any kind of special treatment.

"It's fine," I said, following him out. "I probably need to work on Bernard a little harder."

"Yeah, yeah, it's great stuff. I've been using that monologue for over ten years now. It still breaks me up. It's like jazz; every time I hear it I notice something new that wasn't there before. Have you ever heard me play the piano? I play the piano really beautifully."

"Yes. I have. You're very good."

We now stood in front of his car. He threw his stuff in the backseat while I leaned against the door, trying to squeeze something more out of our last few minutes of time together.

"Thanks, Stan." I never called him Dad, although I was sure he would have wanted me to, if only for other people to hear. The term "dad" didn't exactly roll off my tongue. In my mind, I didn't like the false intimacy that the word implied to someone I was just getting to know and had such mixed feelings about, but sometimes I did use the word in my head, just to test it out, find its nuance, like "Bernard."

"So, how's your mother?"

"She's good. I talked to her this morning. She's happy I'm taking your class."

Unless we were talking about comedy, we couldn't have a conversation for longer than a few minutes without his turning it into a rant, usually directed at one of the scores of people who had wronged him; often he wanted to bring up my mother to let me know what a difficult woman she'd been to deal with and why it hadn't worked between them. You'd think their divorce had become final the week before instead of nearly two decades earlier.

"You know, your mother is a very intelligent woman, and very funny." It was like a follow-the-dots; I knew right where he was taking this.

"I know."

"But she just didn't respect me. She thought she knew everything and she didn't want to learn, which is too bad."

"Mmhmm."

"And Gil, he's a derelict." My relationship with my stepfather was troubled at best, but still, it was a little like the pot calling the kettle a deadbeat dad. I tried to turn the conversation back to more neutral ground.

"I've been writing some jokes that I'd love to try out next week if I can."

"I'm glad you're taking my class, Stef. I see some real potential. You could learn a lot from me. With my help you might be able to get up onstage."

The following week in class Stan's students took turns working out new material in front of the room. I was nervous, knowing I'd get a chance to try out some jokes I'd been working on in front of an actual audience. Each of us had five or ten minutes, which we were to treat like a live performance, right down to the "good to be here"s, "where are you from"s, and "I almost didn't make it here tonight . . ."s. This was by far my favorite part of class, like tinkering in the comedy design studio before the final product was ever seen by the public. Even before I'd written my own jokes, I loved being part of the process, like I was in a secret society. Davey, a Dudley Moore–ish type, tried his new bit about what mall cops talk about in the locker room after their shift: "Man, big trouble today at Swirlz. I risked my life trying their new lemon yogurt." I imagined this is what congressmen must feel like when they sit in on classified White House briefings. Carter, a menschy towering black man, capped his set with "In my hometown there was a homeless man named

Old Tom, who lived in a condemned shack. When Old Tom died, they found over forty thousand dollars under his mattress . . . If he had only looked under his mattress!" It was an instant hit. I was right where I wanted to be.

When it was my turn I was nervous, but I remembered the things Stan had taught me—I stood on the stage, owning the space surrounding me, willing myself to exude a "wait till they hear this" vibe instead of fearing their reaction. "I get hit on all the time. But the thing that really drives me nuts is every guy uses the exact same pickup line. I'll be talking to a guy for one minute and right away I get, 'Do you want a mint?' Guys, I've heard that one a million times. Be original." I told the joke slowly and deliberately, building until it hit a crescendo into the punch line, which paid off with the best part of all: laughter. And then, reassured by the great response, I started again. "In Los Angeles, people always want to compare you to a celebrity. Like everywhere I go people think I look like Cindy Crawford. [pause] They don't say it *out loud*, but I know that's what they're thinking. Hey, if enough people put it out there, who am I to deny it?" The joke got a laugh and I continued, making sure to appreciate the absurdity of my own act and to be amused by it during my performance.

It was by far the best I'd ever felt. I'd done it, accomplished it, been brave. But there was something else: I felt a kinship with Stan because I felt that now we had something tangible in common. We could really get each other.

Afterward, Stanley and I had our talk again while he was packing his things. "You can't teach funny. Some of my students don't have the stuff. They're just not funny and they'll never be funny, but what am I going to do, not take their money?" He seemed irritated, personally insulted at the idea of someone who lacked innate humor having the audacity to be interested in a career in comedy. "But I see it in you; you were born funny—you're my kid, it's in the genes." This was music to my ears.

"I was going to go to Yesterdays in Westwood on Tuesday and sign up for the open mic night with some of the other guys," I said tentatively. "I really want to see if I can do it."

"Oh no! You're not ready for that. It takes a long time to do that."

"But it's just an open mic. No one expects a professional level of comedy there. It's not for money or anything, just to learn, to get over my fear. All your students do them." My feelings were definitely hurt.

"You've got a long way to go before you could be part of the Flying Handelmans. But stick with me, stick with this class, and I'll teach you everything I know." I'd been taking Stanley's class because I knew I wanted to do stand-up comedy. I'd caught the stand-up bug, which for me turned out to be chronic and impossible to shake, much like TB. I knew I wanted to perform in a comedy club like the others. I was ready to be a part of this and stop watching everything from the safety of the seats. There were lessons to be learned in this class, or these funny people wouldn't keep coming back every week and paying my father their rent money for the indelible wisdom I'd heard he could impart, but I was convinced that if I didn't start performing on my own like the others, I wouldn't be able to relate the training to myself.

"I want to try this. I think I could be good," I said quietly, not wanting to draw attention to it, not sure it sounded believable.

"Well, if you want to perform, I'll tell you what, why don't I let you use some of my act? It's a good act. You can work on learning it in class. It's a dynamite act, Stef. You can't go wrong. Use any lines you like."

"That's a very nice offer, Stan." And it *was* a nice offer. It was all he had left to give, and I was grateful that he wanted to give it to me. "But I want to do my own stuff. I have a different style."

"I can't support that. You aren't ready to perform. You need more training," he said. *You need me* is what he didn't say. After a career and marriages that hadn't gone as planned, at that moment I was the sum total of what he had to show for himself, and if I went out on my own, he might not get credit. So the question was, as talented and brilliant as I did believe he was, was I going to be a franchise or an original? It was actually a tough call, because maybe I couldn't do it.

"I'm going to go on Tuesday. Maybe I'll see you there. And thanks . . . Dad." I didn't know if I'd ever call him Dad again. I sort of doubted it, but I didn't want to take it back either. In that moment it was the truth, and so I hoped that it sounded believable. At least more believable than "Bernard."

Two and Two

Before stalking was technically illegal, and well before Google made it all so innocent, I once saw a guy I liked on TV and made it my full-time job to meet him and make him my husband. The show was *Love Connection,* hosted by arguably the hottest Republican game show host in my not-so-limited viewing experience. In 1986, otherwise known as "back in the day," before dating shows were all about how many people you could transmit a venereal disease to in the least amount of time, *Love Connection* ruled. *Love Connection* was an innocent show full of people who genuinely were seeking love, not just their fifteen minutes of skankdom, and I was *obsessed* with it.

I wanted nothing more than to appear on the show, get hooked up with the man of my dreams, and share

every sordid detail about my date with America. At
this point in my life I'd yet to learn about boundaries
(some might argue that I still haven't, but those people
are uptight a-holes and I could probably take each and
every one of them in a fight*) and I was ripe to be on
reality television. The only hitch in my plan was that,
according to the producers, I was too young. In those
days you had to be twenty-three to sign away all your
rights to your image, and although I was dying to do
just that, I was twenty. Three years seemed way too
long to wait for televised love, and I wasn't adept at
faking birth certificates yet, so I was forced to just enjoy
the show from the isolation of my living room and
continue trying to meet men the old-fashioned way.

Meeting cute guys on purpose was exhausting; I had
to tease my hair, lacquer on enough Aqua Net to turn
the ozone into Swiss cheese, squeeze into some zipper-
ankle jeans and a neon top, and head to the Red Onion
for happy hour. Even though drinks were cheap during
happy hour, I had to pre-drink at home to combat

---

* Inserted strictly for bravado. The author actually doubts she could
take most of you. Especially the mean, wiry, and tricky bitches. You
know who you are.

the getting-carded jitters. I'd secured a fake ID a few years back from Gayle Price, a woman I worked with at Burger King. The problem was it was Gayle's welfare ID, it was expired, and it looked nothing like me. I'd really hit the bad fake ID trifecta, so I had to be feeling a special kind of cocky to try to pass it off as me. It was highly stressful. Sometimes I'd get into character by three p.m. if I knew I was going out that night. I'd answer only to Gayle and I'd eat only snacks I could buy with food stamps, figuring surplus cheese, cocktail weenies, and a Coors Light would sound like the perfect poor-person's lunch in the event I was quizzed on it by a wily doorman. I didn't want to take any chances because getting turned away at the door was nothing short of humiliating.

I didn't go to bars for the dancing or even for the drinking; I went out for the sole purpose of meeting the man of my 1986 dreams. In hindsight, my quest may have bordered on insane desperation if you want to get technical about it . . . or talk to some of the men I dated back then. It's just that I so badly wanted to meet someone who would be a perfect match for me, someone who got my jokes, someone cute—no mustaches, please—smart, and kind, and someone who liked the same music I did. It's not easy to find a straight guy who's willing to lie in bed and listen to the theme from *Tootsie* over and over with you. Actually it's not possible. And really, maybe it shouldn't be possible; some things aren't meant to be shared. Needless to say, I hadn't met this mythical funny, straight-yet-soft-rock-loving man in the bars, which is why I was driven to stalking when I spied my future husband on an episode of *Love Connection*.

The episode of destiny started out like any other. First we were introduced to Andrea, who'd gotten the coveted role of "chooser." She was a bottle blonde from San Gabriel Valley in a skimpy baby doll dress who looked like she was a girl who would describe a pair of boots as "kicky!" and who definitely owned a pink purse and a picture frame that says "Best Friends Forever." If it had been fifteen years later she'd have been Jessica Simpson. She was way too bubbly and annoying for my taste but, hey, some guys dig that.

Andrea had three videos of men to choose from. This was my favorite part of the show because I loved to watch the snippets of video they showed the viewers and make my choice, then get super-excited if the "chooser" picked my choice so I could go on a date

with them vicariously. My new boyfriend on this episode was the first video clip shown. My first glimpse of
him was in a video freeze-frame, his face oddly stopped
in midsentence while host Chuck Woolery gave us the
basics: "First we have Greg; he's twenty-three and is a
photographer from Los Angeles who has a funny way
of showing a woman he's interested." Then they cut to
my boyfriend.

"If I'm into a girl, I'll let them drive my car on the
date. It's a trust thing. Oh, and any woman who can
drive a stick shift gets a second date. That's sexy."

There was instant chemistry. I drove a stick shift. In
fact, I learned to drive on a stick shift and was forced
to take my driver's license test in our car with manual
transmission. So far I'd never seen the fruits of my
labor. No one had ever been *attracted* to me for knowing my way around a clutch, but now that I thought
about it, it was high time they were. This guy was very
cute and very my type: brown eyes, baby face, twinkly
eyes—just a hint of bad boy. He did have long hair
and I wasn't normally a fan, but I decided that I would
make an exception for Greg. Personality had to start
counting for something. Life was about risks—risks
coupled with detangler.

Next up was Justin, who mumbled something

about liking a woman who would cook for him, and then the third guy was Curt, whose greatest ambition in life was to be a successful reggae musician. I suspected that the closest he'd get would be having a bong shop in Jamaica, New York. But I magnanimously wished him luck.

"Andrea, why don't you tell us who you picked?" Chuck said while I nervously ate through my third bowl of air-popped popcorn drizzled with Tabasco sauce. I'd recently been told by a black guy that I had a great ass and had immediately gone on a crash diet consisting solely of popcorn and Diet Sprite.

"I chose Greg," Andrea said, and both the studio audience and I broke into a round of applause.

"Okay," Chuck said. "Greg's with us backstage. Greg?" Unlike today's voyeuristic dating shows, where we get to see the couples in action in their hot tubs and on their helicopter rides, on *Love Connection*, where they just reported back, we were forced to trust their recollection. Greg's face popped up on the big monitor, looking even cuter than on his video. I knew we made the right decision.

"Hi, Chuck."

"So, Greg, what was your first impression of Andrea?"

"I thought she seemed great. Very pretty. Nice smile." Chuck turned to Andrea.

"And, Andrea, what did you think when you first met Greg?" Andrea made a face like she'd just heard the news that truffles are a type of fungus. "I was surprised. He seemed a little different in person. Not quite my usual type." Obviously they were off to a bad start. This show never had any dates that were so-so; either it was pure rapture or they were at each other's throats. That was just fine with me. Greg was definitely *my* type.

"Okay, Andrea, tell us about the date."

Andrea complained about everything at the restaurant Greg took her to, from the décor down to the valet's cologne, and explained that she personally preferred a more expensive dining option and she needed a guy who made more money. Greg looked pained but didn't argue back. He'd never win anyway. I knew her type: typical LA high-maintenance bimbo—no doubt an actress and not a fitness trainer like she claimed. Right then and there I decided I'd have to find this guy and introduce him to the exciting and wonderful world of lovable broke brunettes.

I could barely contain my excitement through the ad break, so I dialed up some friends to turn on *Love Connection* so they could take a look at my future husband. My friend Claudia picked up on the first ring and together we waited for the commercials to finish. Finally Greg came back on-screen for his gripping take on the night in question. "Greg, what happened after dinner?" Chuck asked. "Did you let her drive your car?"

"I offered," Greg said. Of course he did. *She's not worth it, Greg.*

"He does this thing where he drums on the steering wheel when he's driving," Andrea said. Why was she still there? I was completely over her at this point. "He keeps real drumsticks in his car, which I found weird. At this point I just wanted to go home." Of course she did. It had been four hours since she'd had her roots dyed.

"My God, he deserves better than this twat," I said to Claudia, who was still hanging on the phone with me.

The date ended and it was time to see who the audience had chosen for Andrea. If it was Greg, the show would pay for them to have a second date if they both agreed. If it was another guy, she could stay with Greg and they'd be on their own, or she could date the audience's choice and get money for the date. Shockingly to me, the audience had chosen the reggae dude.

It sort of made sense to me though, because I never went for the obvious choice. When *The Hardy Boys* was on, I was in love with Parker Stevenson while all my friends wanted Shaun Cassidy. Or on *Love Boat,* while everyone lusted over the handsome feather-banged guest star, I was having lewd thoughts about Doc. In my defense, knee socks could not obscure the legs on Bernie Kopell. Greg and I would laugh about this later. As would our children. And our children's children. Because life is funny.

"Claudia, I've got to go. I need to find him."

"Are you serious?" she asked in a way that told me she wanted no part of my psychosis. But I was in love.

"I've never been more serious. How many Greg Wildings [not his real name] can there be in Los Angeles?" (Back in those days they often used people's first and last names on TV shows. They also used real seven-digit telephone numbers—none of that five-five-five bullshit like now. Apparently people like me would call those real numbers and the real people who live at the houses attached to those numbers would get mad.)

Unfortunately for me, there were quite a few Greg Wildings (still not his real name) in the city of Los

Angeles, so I had a few rum and Cokes for bravery and then one more for fun, and I started pushing buttons. The first Greg sounded eighty, so I hung up and had another rum and Coke. Around twenty minutes and fourteen messages later, I felt I'd done what I could. The rest was up to fate.

"Hi, is this Stefanie?" a cute-sounding guy asked the next day when I answered the phone on the first ring.

"Um, no. Whom may I say is calling?" I asked, half-wary that this was a bill collector, half freaking the fuck out that it was my destiny on the line.

"This is Greg." *Oh no it is not Greg calling me!* I was sober and suddenly way more shy. Greg was curious as to how I'd gotten his number but otherwise sounded downright charmed and we proceeded to make a plan. He would be coming over to my apartment that very day to meet me.

Immediately, excitement was spiked by anxiety. What was I doing? I didn't even know this guy; he could be a mass-murderer. He was a photographer, after all. What if he told me that our Hot Ladies of the Eighties calendar was going to be shot on some remote dry lake bed, where he ended up killing me (after getting some great shots, naturally) and leaving me in the trunk of his car? I wasn't one to turn down a modeling opportunity if one presented itself, so I knew I'd have to go with him (after all, I hadn't moved all the way to Los Angeles to *turn down* modeling jobs), but I figured I should have a safety net in place. I called Claudia. "Greg's headed over here, and I just want you to know that in case something happens to me."

"Wait, Greg's coming over to your apartment?"

"Yes. I called him yesterday and he called me back and now he's coming over."

"Whoa. I can't believe you actually called him," Claudia said.

"Claudia, in this life, you need to make things happen. But listen, if he decides to take some modeling shots of me and something happens, I want someone to know that I'm with him."

"Why would he take modeling shots of you? Did he say he was going to? Is he even that kind of photographer?"

"Why *wouldn't* he take modeling shots of me?" Claudia was getting on my nerves. It was typical of her to try to undercut me. If I lived through this date

I vowed to find some more supportive friends. "Look, I'm not on trial here. I just don't want to rule anything out."

"Hi," Greg said when I opened the door. He stood in front of me—all five feet of him. I knew the camera adds ten pounds but I guess it also adds ten inches. But what was more disconcerting was that he had a very large head. It might have worked out if he was an oddly great-looking little guy the way that guy from *The Station Agent* was, but *The Station Agent* was still seventeen years from being made, and this was not that guy. In that moment, the obvious questions were running through my mind: Was it rude to ask someone their hat size? Was he officially a little person or just short? Did he have to sit on a phone book when he drove?

"Can I come in?" he asked. He was like a thinner version of Danny DeVito but minus the charisma and with a much bigger head. I kind of needed a minute to readjust my expectations but I ushered him in the door. I certainly didn't want to seem shallow. After all, I'd tracked him down and now he was here without a second thought—which made sense when you thought about it. *Of course* he responded to some random crazy

girl's drunken answering machine message; he was desperate! I suddenly envied Andrea, who at that moment
was probably high as a kite on hydroponic weed, listening to Jimmy Cliff albums with her new Rastafarian
boyfriend with a normal-size head. *Maybe I should
track* her *down to tell her this story,* I thought.

Greg and I sat on my couch and struggled for conversation. I tried not to sneak a peek to see if his feet
could touch the ground, but it was a losing battle (they
did, barely). Greg, however, seemed to have no aware-
ness of my drunk-dialer's remorse. In fact, he seemed
kind of cocky and, could it be, less than enraptured
with me! I nervously checked a reflection to see if my
jeans flattered my ass. I was self-conscious pondering
the nerve of this shallow little man! Maybe the fact that
I had a good five inches on him was throwing him off,
but he almost seemed like he wanted to leave.

"I'm on my way to brunch at the Celebrity Centre,"
he threw out like it was absolutely the most normal
thing in the world. "If you like, I'd love for you to come
along." The Celebrity Centre was the main hangout for
Scientologists in Hollywood. This was very bad news;
he wasn't going to slaughter me on a dry lake bed. Oh
no, it was much more sinister than that; he was going
to try to indoctrinate me into the Church of Scientol-

ogy. Worse still, if I refused to go to the Church of Scientology he'd suspect it was because of his physical appearance and then he'd think I was superficial and not just terrified of cults and also kind of superficial.

"I hear great things about Scientology," I told him, trying to figure a plan to get out of this with no one's feelings hurt. "I hear that if I become a Scientologist I can double my income . . . oh wait, maybe it's if I double my income I can become a Scientologist." Scientology was a fairly expensive spiritual pursuit from what I understood, and I had no intention of spending the last sixty dollars I had to my name to get hooked up to an e-meter. I had better things to spend my money on, like alcohol. "Thank you so much for the offer but I have a prior commitment today," I said wanly.

"Okay, how about next week?" he said. "I'll even let you drive."

"Sure," I said. "But I don't know how to drive a stick."

Studs

"Who's the celebrity you most want to do?" The executive producer in charge of the *Studs* audition was grilling a wannabe contestant while I tried not to noticeably wince.

"Pam Anderson, like that other dude said. She's smokin' hot." These were not my kinda people but I was stuck here, so I had to play along. He said it as if it was a news flash to the room, but in reality he was the fourth guy in a row to answer "Pam Anderson." I was starting to feel like having brown hair was akin to having herpes. Not one guy had mentioned Shannen Doherty, which was the closest celebrity I could figure was sort of like me: dark hair and a grouchy attitude.

The cramped, overheated office in the television production building was wall-to-wall with twentysomethings ranging in attractiveness from "so so" to "oh *hell* no." When I made up my mind to audition for *Studs,* I had no intention of actually going on the show; at least that's what I told myself. Ever since *Love Connection,* I'd had an unnatural obsession with dating shows, at once repulsed and fascinated by people who looked for love in such a public manner. And now that I was old enough to do it, I was sure I'd moved beyond wanting to.

I was in the room because I intended to write a magazine article about what really went on in a casting call for a dating show. I was there as a journalist, deep inside the audition process, to get better access to behind-the-scenes secrets. I was there to satisfy the nation's burning right to know what was really going on with these exhibitionist singles of Los Angeles. Okay, no one had "officially" hired me to write this article, but once it was completed, I was sure there would be a bidding war. But for now, as uncomfortable as I was, it was clear I was too far along to just up and leave.

I'd already been required to fill out more paperwork than I imagine is necessary to join the military. Name, age, job, best quality, worst quality, bad habits, qualities you look for in a mate, turn-ons, turnoffs, pet peeves, have you ever committed a crime? Why do you want to be on a dating show? The list went on and on. I half expected to be subjected to a physical and I was quietly relieved that I'd showered and put on clean undies for this.

I answered the questions on the application as honestly as I possibly could because I was worried I might be quizzed later and I didn't want to have to memorize my fake responses. I was already nervous enough about being there under false pretenses.

Some of the wannabe contestants had brought headshots and held them anxiously in their laps like defendants in small-claims court waiting to spring up and hand the bailiff their receipts. They were taking this opportunity very seriously. I didn't have a headshot with me; instead I opted to just let them snap a Polaroid of me standing against the wall.

This was the early nineties, a time when men grew out their hair and wore skintight jeans and 400 cc boob jobs were becoming as common as Labrador retrievers. The guys in the room were all hopped up on testosterone and ingestible acne meds and called each other "dude" every six seconds. The producer in charge of this was a striking, businesslike black woman named Jasmine. One by one we'd have to get up and stand in front of her for questioning, and she'd go over the application we'd turned in earlier.

The man now standing in the center of the room getting grilled was named Jack, and he sported a big yellow bandana around his head à la Latin pop star Gerardo. I immediately nicknamed him Rico Suave in my head. I'm sure he thought he looked like the lead singer of a glam metal band with his laced-up-to-the-knees black boots and faux snakeskin pants, but I thought he looked like a bisexual pirate. If he'd had a big parrot on his shoulder that squawked the answers to all of Jasmine's questions no one would've blinked an eye. His face had a weathered look that brought to mind someone who'd been shipwrecked on an island for ten years without sunscreen; turns out he just lived in Marina del Rey.

"So Pam Anderson? That's your woman?"

"I'd do her," Rico Suave said blandly, as if he actually expected the opportunity to present itself anytime and he had to think it over.

I leaned over to the girl sitting on my right and whispered, "Who says shit like that? Doesn't he make you want to hurl?" I needed some camaraderie but I was barking up the wrong tree.

"I love this show," she whispered. "And this guy's *hot*."

I looked back at Rico. I'd seen hotter Q-tips. Had

this girl gotten tipsy before the audition? It was the only explanation I could come up with for finding anyone in this room attractive, not to mention the only way to account for her outfit. I could basically see the pink flesh of her breasts peeking out from underneath a cropped baby doll T-shirt that could only have been from the toddler section of Baby Gap. For all of our safety, I hoped she wouldn't need to raise her hand. I pegged her as being the sort of girl who'd seen her share of roadie penis.

Rico Suave was going over his prison record now with Jasmine. "It was my second DUI so I ended up spending the night downtown," he told her, recounting the story as if the DUI had just been the missing piece of the puzzle that made him a total catch. Pretty soon we'd heard more about the Bi Pirate than we needed to: he used to be a lawyer who had his own plane, but since the DUIs he'd quit law and was a full-time beach bum. But, he made sure to point out, he still had his own plane.

"Who in this room turns you on?" Jasmine asked him. He scanned the chairs, taking his time to eye-rape every woman in the room, finally settling on the woman next to me.

"She's doable," he said in a voice that made me

want to take a Silkwood shower. Baby Gap leaned over to me and said, "Oh my God, he has his own plane."

"I hope Captain Morgan isn't his copilot," I whispered back.

Unbelievably I was next.

"So it says here that your biggest turn-on is a guy with a sense of humor," the producer said slowly, looking up from my application. "Does size matter?"

"Size of his sense of humor?" I asked with sincere confusion.

"Size of his *package*. Size of his pack-age." The producer repeated it, enunciating the two syllables in case I didn't get it. I had to keep reminding myself I wasn't there to go on the show. It didn't matter. I would never go out with anyone in this room. Who cared? So why was I worried that I needed lipstick?

"The celebrity you want to sleep with is Kevin Nealon? Is that a joke?" Jasmine stared me down. The girls in the room were outnumbered by about three to one and we'd already had a few Johnny Depps and a Brad Pitt, so I guessed that maybe that was the first time Kevin Nealon's name had been brought up in a sexual way at a game show audition. I briefly second-guessed myself but decided that Kevin Nealon was an absolutely valid choice. He was hilarious on *SNL,* tall, and even sorta good-looking. My normal type was nerdy Jewish guys, so I figured Kevin Nealon would be more palatable for these people. I'd actually contemplated writing down Woody Allen but I didn't want to make a spectacle of myself.

The producer continued putting me through my paces for a few more minutes and eventually got to her favorite question: who here would you do? I'd had plenty of time to suss out the situation and decided that I'd rather repeat junior high school twice than go to first base with anyone in that room. But I made a show of slowly looking around the room, finally stopping at Rico Suave, pointing at him dramatically, and saying in a ridiculous voice, "He's . . . doable." It got a laugh, except from Rico, who I think now assumed we were dating.

The rest of the people eagerly took their turn in front of Jasmine, answering questions without a hint of humor or levity, happy to be part of, included, one of the crowd. They looked so easy in their own fake 'n' bake tanned skin while I felt like I was crawling out of mine. While the last of the female wannabe contestants reported her turn-ons ("Wearing lingerie for my man") and turnoffs ("Bad breath! Yuck!") I reminded myself that I was there for the story and that thankfully I'd never have to see any of these people again.

Then, as our hormonal cattle call was pointed toward the door, I was one of a handful who were held back. I'd made it to the callback. It was a dubious honor. I have no idea why I agreed. And even less idea why I was secretly thrilled.

At the next level of the audition matrix, I couldn't help but let a few optimistic thoughts creep in. A couple of these people seemed *almost* normal. The room was free of any overt freaks, and thankfully there was no sign or scent of Rico Suave. In fact, they seemed to have culled the more cheese-free candidates from the preliminary interviews, judging by a couple of seemingly datable guys in the room. Was it possible they'd have a Kevin Nealon type in their Rolodex of eligible contestants? I wondered. A Kevin Nealon type who specifically requested a Shannen Doherty type? Okay, more realistically a Gabrielle Carteris type with a slightly disdainful exterior masking a deeply insecure yet impossibly generous heart.

But this was still *Studs,* so I suspected that at least

a Members Only jacket and more than one cold sore probably lurked around every corner. My guard stayed up. Still, I played along with all the questions posed to me. Even though I was there on assignment, I figured I should at least see this callback through. I didn't want to be suspected of being a spy. I told a funny story of a date that had gone awry, and I laughed at dumb things the other wannabes said, just to show that I could play well with others. I trained myself to act very open-minded . . . almost like I wasn't counting the minutes until I could immerse myself in Purell. Just before we left, we were told that if they found a show for us, we'd get a call soon.

The call came sooner than I expected. Two days later, Jasmine was on the line to let me know that I'd been "matched" with two "hot" guys. She stressed that I'd need to call them and set up a date *as soon as possible* so I could have both dates done in time for a taping the *following week*. After my dates I'd be speaking to a producer about what I thought of the guys so they could come up with ridiculous quotes from me, like "His body had more definition than Webster's dictionary."

Suddenly my little fantasy had crossed the center line and was veering dangerously into reality. But I had convinced myself that I was in it for the story. The lid on horny TV bachelors wouldn't blow itself off. So strictly for journalistic purposes, I figured I'd call the first guy, José, to see what he was all about. I called him in the middle of the afternoon hoping to just leave a message. But he picked up the phone on the sixth ring sounding like I'd just roused him from a long siesta. He told me he was a barista, rolling his "r" as he uttered the word with a proud flourish, and it started to make perfect sense. This being the very early nineties, I didn't know that "barista" was a fancy way of saying he worked at Starbucks. I simply deduced from his name and accent that he was from Spain, and from the fancy-sounding job that he had to be rich. A sexy Spanish rich barrrista—mmmmm, yes, please! *This could definitely work for me,* I found myself musing.

I suggested an authentic little taco stand for our first date—a place called Paquito Mas. Technically it's Mexican food, but Spain, Mexico—same difference, I figured. I deliberately chose to go low-key on our first outing together to show him that I wasn't materialistic and only attracted to him for his wealth. Obviously, once we were a couple we'd travel constantly, splitting our time between the States and his beach house in Barcelona, where we'd drink sangria out of hand-blown glass pitchers on a sunny terrace with its breathtaking view of the ocean. I imagined he'd probably wear a Speedo, but I'd forgive him because he's European, after all, and that's just part of their culture. I wondered briefly if this meant I'd have to wear those insanely tiny string bikinis that looked like ass floss and if so, how soon I'd have to get a Brazilian.

Since I was on a roll, I decided to recharge with some rice cakes and Nutella and then dive right into my next call, to Jackson. Unfortunately, while fantasizing about my future with José, I accidentally polished off the entire tub of Nutella, and when I read the fat content per serving and multiplied that by total servings, I realized I'd just consumed 110 grams of fat. I considered this a bad omen.

As I was coming to terms with this caloric intake and its likely impact on the scope of my impending Brazilian wax, Jackson answered on the first ring with a loud "Yello!"

"Hi, is this Jackson?"

"You got him."

"Hi, it's Stefanie calling from *Studs*. I got your number from the show. How's it going?"

"Well, heeeeey, you," he said in a voice I felt I'd heard somewhere before. "I was waiting to get your call." This was sort of weird since I'd been given his number only a few hours ago. It seemed to me that I was showing a lot of initiative by calling as soon as I did. "I've already heard from the other lady."

"Oh," is all I could think of to say.

"So what do you look like? Are you blond?"

"Not exactly," I said, possibly slightly defensively. "Not even a little bit. I have dark brown hair."

"Huh." He wasted no time before asking his next question. "What do you do for exercise?" he asked, meaning, "Are you a fatty?" I was trying very hard to get past the whole Nutella unpleasantness in my mind and this wasn't helping. Jackson had a way of asking questions that made me feel attacked.

"Well, walking is considered exercise, right?"

"Do you belong to a gym?" Either I was being oversensitive or this guy was a dick.

"Am I on the stand here?" I shot back with a little laugh, because I didn't want to seem like a bitch but I needed to stop this line of questioning. It seemed to work.

"Sorry, babe. I used to be a lawyer." By now, more than the Nutella was making me feel icky.

"Oh, so what do you do now?"

"Now who's the lawyer?" He laughed uproariously. "I'm just kidding, babe. I'm totally busting you. Just hanging out doing the beach bum thing. I made a crapload of money in the eighties." I got a sickening feeling in the pit of my stomach. This just couldn't be. Jasmine wouldn't, would she? But then again, she was a television producer, and television producers are known to be a bit sleazy.

"Do you have your own plane, Jack?" I asked, feeling the Nutella rising back up.

"Whaa? You know me! How do you know me?" *Oh God, this can't be.*

"Rico Suave. You set me up with Rico *fucking* Suave," I practically yelled into the phone when Jasmine finally called me back. I'd left her two messages letting her know I would not under any circumstances be going on either of my dates. If she'd set me up with Gerardo, God only knew how bad José would be. Clearly she took me for a woman with no standards. I hadn't expected her to spend a week finding the delicate balance of a man who was at once strong enough to stand up to me yet manly and evolved enough to let me be the strong one sometimes, a man who could make me laugh even when I was crying over a situation at work—like the one I'd been in last week where I got

suspended from my job for two days for serving a
customer a piece of Death by Chocolate cake that had
accidentally fallen on the floor for like a millisecond,
but another customer had seen me do it and told the
manager; a man who would whisk me off to Europe
to pop the question when we'd been dating for just
over a year and insist that we have a baby straightaway
because he's always dreamed of being a father. Okay,
I hadn't expected her to find perfection, but I had
expected her to put in a little effort. This was my life
we were talking about. Wasn't I worth that?

"Stefanie, calm down. It seemed like you two kind
of had a thing going on. We normally don't fix people
up who have already seen each other in the room but I
thought it would be a good match. It seemed like you
liked him."

"What? How?"

"You picked him out as the person who turns you
on." Jasmine was clearly not a fan of irony. "Look,
Jack's a great guy. He owns his own plane. It's just a
date."

"I don't care if he owns his own country. I don't
care if he wants to make me the queen of that country.
I'm not going out with him."

"Okay, well we can switch him out and give you

someone else. Will that be okay?" *No, it wouldn't be okay, Jasmine.* It was way too late for apologies.

"I don't think you understand. I'm not going on the dates. I'm not going on the show. The truth is, I'm not even a reality-show-contestant type. I'm not even an actress. I'm a writer!"

"Yeah, you should've been up front before you wasted so much of our time. Now I have to go and find a replacement. But good luck to you." Jasmine sounded pretty irritated but I knew she'd find someone easily considering how many people were in that audition. I prayed it would be the Baby Gap chick, if she wasn't already in the mix—those two deserved each other. The bad news was, I wouldn't be going out with José after all. But I chose to look at the bright side: I wouldn't be needing that Brazilian any time soon.

Driving Miss Bateman

Justine Bateman can fuck herself with her skis. And the same goes for her sister, I thought to myself as I sat in the driver's seat of my limo—scratch that, *town car*—outside of Killer Shrimp waiting for the eighties sitcom star to finish eating her hourlong dinner. She and her sister were taking full advantage of the two-hour ride maximum while I stayed behind in the car starving to death and nursing sore muscles from carrying their ski trip gear the length of Burbank airport and out through the parking garage and loading it into the trunk. It wasn't looking good for me to make a quick drop-off, call dispatch, and grab another client, and it seemed more than likely this would be another twenty-six-dollar day.

I desperately needed a full-body massage after the

crap week I'd had, but obviously I couldn't afford it. So far, I'd received a single paycheck, which was somewhere in the neighborhood of $185—and that was for two weeks' work—after taxes. So I was pulling in about ninety bucks a week, which would have been awesome in *1920,* but it wasn't going to afford me even a decent foot rub in 1994.

To be fair to Justine, it wasn't really her fault. Carrying luggage was part of the driver's job and clients were fully within their rights to make use of their two-hour trip, paid for by the studio, any way they wanted. But sitting around waiting for someone to finish eating an expensive dinner while other drivers were getting assigned the good trips wasn't what I'd signed up for. Driving celebrities around was supposed to be the cool part of the job, the perk, a possible networking opportunity, or so I'd thought when I applied for the job. And to make matters worse, it was becoming clear I'd have to decide between the job and my dog.

I'd shown up at the limo company after seeing an ad in the paper advertising for drivers who could work odd hours. I needed a little time apart from waitressing, but I also required a flexible schedule so I could do stand-up at night and also care for my new puppy. Georgia, a half-pit/half-Lab stray I'd adopted from the pound, was proving to be a major challenge, maybe more than I could handle. Like most relationships, she was turning out to be a completely different mutt from the scruffy, lovable one I'd fallen for when we met. When I first laid eyes on her at the shelter, she'd been downright quiet and coy, which I took to indicate a mellow and sweet disposition. I was naturally excited to take our relationship to the next level. But I now believe she'd been sedated with a heavy dose of doggy Valium. Within a day of moving in with me, her true personality began to show itself. It started with attacking power cords as if she were wrestling pythons, leaving me with very few working appliances, but I told myself she'd calm down and go back to being that lovable pooch that had swept me off my feet.

Within weeks she'd escalated to more troubling behavior, such as growling and aggression toward little children at the dog park. Now, at this point in my life, I was not a huge fan of most of the precious studio-executive spawn who terrorized the parks of the Hollywood Hills, so when I snapped Georgia off her leash and she charged a four-year-old from a hundred yards, pinning him screaming in fear under her paws, I pretended to be horrified even though I was secretly on *her* side. After all, when you really got into the details, who could say who started it? But the parents were not too understanding and we were threatened with a lawsuit if we returned.

I'd also just started dating a new guy and I didn't want something as tedious as a job getting in the way of what little Georgia-free time I had left in my schedule.

When it came to my new career in the prestigious ground transportation industry, I figured I had three big things going for me: 1) I had a perfect driving record, 2) I looked adorable in a chauffeur cap, and 3) I drove a stick. Really the only strike against me going into it was a poor sense of direction and an inability to read a map, but I figured the key to being a good driver was instinct anyway.

When I called the company to see about an interview they just said, "Come in tomorrow and we'll run your driver's license." They didn't specify a time, so to be conscientious I arrived bright and early at noon. After running my license and answering a few perfunctory questions to screen out violent ex-cons and hard-core drug users (they didn't need to hear about the accidental freebasing in my past until at least the company Christmas party), I was offered a job. This did not come as a surprise to me; after so many job interviews, I had the whole process down to a science.

The only glitch? In my zeal to make a good impression, I hadn't blinked an eye when my new boss told me I'd need to arrive for my first day at five a.m.

The next morning it was still dark when I was assigned to ride along with "Big Al," a husky Italian grandpa type who was one of the few drivers trusted to drive a stretch. Big Al was in charge of all of Chevy Chase's transportation. Our limousine company had accounts with the major studios and a broadcast network, so a big chunk of their trade was schlepping celebrities on the studio's tab. I'd heard that Chevy Chase could be difficult to deal with and was possibly a Vicodin addict. "Horseshit," said Big Al when I mentioned the rumors. "I drive the man almost every day and I've never found Mr. Chase to be anything but delightful."

We parked outside of Chevy's gated driveway at six thirty a.m. for a seven a.m. pickup to take him to LAX. From the moment Chevy breezed into the car at seven forty-five a.m., he joked around, engaged us in conversation, and, as I can attest from my constant surveillance in the visor vanity mirror, the man didn't pop a single painkiller. He kept up the banter until we let him out at the Delta terminal approximately twenty minutes later. And then when Big Al handed Chevy his luggage from the trunk, Chevy handed Big Al a fifty-dollar bill.

The base salary for this job was twenty-six dollars for up to two hours for the ride plus tip, and that's where I was sure you could make the serious money. These were celebrities. They had loads of cash and were always looking to leave a good impression. The image of a steady flow of Grants and Hamiltons immediately started me shopping for a new futon in my head. Hadn't I heard somewhere that Nicolas Cage once tipped a waitress a thousand dollars? If I drove someone like that, I'd be set for a month. And once I drove Nic, I'd probably become his regular driver because he'd feel comfortable only with me. Also, once he got to talking to me, he'd probably give me a line or two in a movie, not because I *constantly nagged* him about it but because he's a truly giving person and wants to see others succeed. This would be the type of thing that would end up being a great story in the paper for him, and I'd be sure to spread the word about exactly how I got my start in the business: Nic Cage threw me a bone! He's a great guy! Go see all his movies!

"Thanks a lot, guys," Chevy said, walking toward the automatic glass terminal door. "Great talking to you, Stefanie. And a great pleasure as always, Big Al."

Are you fucking kidding me? I thought. *Chevy Chase and I are on a first-name basis.*

The whole Chevy Chase trip took less than thirty minutes, and right then and there it was clear I'd stumbled upon the most brilliant part-time job ever. *Why don't more people do this for a living?* I wondered. It was truly baffling. This limo-driver gig was like the best-kept secret in Hollywood. As far as I was concerned, I'd already wasted way too much time working my ass off in restaurants when I could've been hobnobbing with the rich and famous and getting paid for it. This was like being a personal trainer, minus all the annoying exercise.

Back at the fleet garage I was introduced to the old-timers, who were hanging out, playing pinball in the lounge, smoking Camels, and drinking cup after cup of burned coffee from a pot that looked like it hadn't been cleaned since hitchhiking was safe. I flopped down in an orange and green plaid stuffed armchair in serious need of reupholstering and shut my eyes. After all, I was typically not due to be awake for another few hours. "Why are *you* wanting to drive for a living, little missy?" a man named Carol asked. *Why are* you *still going with the name Carol now that you're a grown man and can make your own decisions?* I thought to myself.

"Why not?" I answered. "It seems pretty cool so far."

"Driving isn't a joke, it's a career, and we take our work very seriously," said another grouch, named Ortiz, who was really old, at least forty.

"I give you a week," said another oldster, Barbara, not looking up from her knitting. Barbara was the fleet garage's older, crankier, liver-spotted answer to Elaine from *Taxi*. This was incredibly insulting to me since I'd had plenty of jobs in my day for slightly longer than *two weeks*. I didn't need this type of negativity.

These geezers weren't exactly rolling out the red carpet for me, but I was going to prove them wrong. I took this *very* seriously. Any job that required little to no effort yet yielded good monetary gain was a job I took extremely seriously.

"I plan to work very hard. My new puppy, Georgia, is depending on me," I announced, hoping to get the room on my side. Barbara suddenly changed personalities.

"I have a cat named Miss Jingles," she said. "She's clairvoyant!" I had no idea how to respond to that.

"Wow. Clairvoyance is a very special gift," I said, happy to bond with the only other woman in the room even if it was suddenly clear she was the victim of too many recreational drugs and not enough mood-stabilizing ones. I mentally switched her *Taxi* character from Elaine to Reverend Jim.

"I'm knitting Miss Jingles a sweater," Barbara said. "Maybe I'll knit one for your doggy too. Have you noticed any psychic abilities?"

"She's quite possibly a fire starter," I said.

An hour later, Big Al and I were out on another celebrity run, this time to fetch Nastassja Kinski, most famous to me for appearing in *Cat People,* which I'd seen no less than ten times. I had to keep pinching myself because I couldn't believe my luck in scoring this job.

We zoomed back to LAX and Big Al taught me a shortcut involving La Brea so that we could avoid the 405 if there was traffic. We made it there faster than I ever have on my own and parked our limo in front of baggage terminal 5 to wait for Nastassja. I was slightly disappointed that we weren't going to wait for her at the gate, but Big Al said that she had a "handler" who would walk her to baggage claim and then bring her outside to meet her car. That would mean I would have no need to wear my cap or hold my sign.

This ride went smoothly as well and I was thrilled

for Big Al when he showed me another fifty-dollar
bill. "That's awesome, Al," I said. I wondered if Nastassja was still spending royalties from her naked snake
poster; who cared as long as she was spreading the
wealth?

"Don't worry, this'll be you before you know it."

I came home from work that day and I was greeted
by a huge pile of poop just inside the front door: a
very succinct memo to me from Georgia regarding my
long hours. To further illustrate the seriousness of my
inconsiderate attitude, she'd also peed in the hallway,
the upstairs bathroom, and about five places in the
living room that I could see, plus a few more that I
could only smell. I wondered if people who adopted
children have to go through this kind of difficult
transition.

If I was going to have to work long hours at this
job, I would have to hire a dog walker to come in once
a day and take her out. This was one of the downsides
to apartment living—no backyard. Well, that and a
loud and chronic masturbator who shared a common
wall with my kitchen. A dog walker was going to cost
me money I didn't have, considering I hadn't actually
driven anyone on my own yet, and doggie day care was
completely out of the question—I didn't trust people

I don't know to be raising my pet. I suddenly had a lot more empathy for single mothers—especially mothers of children with ADHD. *We bust our asses taking care of everyone else, but who supports us?* I thought in a moment of solidarity. If the opportunity and a little downtime presented themselves, I'd definitely do some sort of march or bake sale for this very important cause—at the very least we needed a ribbon. I made a mental note to see which colors were still available.

For now, though, I'd have to lock Georgia in my bedroom, leaving her with the run of my nightly retreat and a tiny bathroom, thus diminishing the potential for disaster.

On my first solo run in a town car—the big limos were for only extremely experienced drivers—I was sent to get Lolita Davidovich from the Warner Bros. lot and take her home. My instruction sheet told me that Lolita was not approved for car phone privileges. Back then the only cell phones invented so far were slightly larger than an iron and were carried around only by presidents of small countries—the rest of the rich used car phones. This meant that the company paying for her ride was not willing to pick up the bill for any expensive phone minutes. It also meant that she was not considered a very big star. But *I'd* heard of her, which was enough for me to feel the thrill of victory. I'd been given a real live celebrity.

Lolita had major attitude from the moment she got in. Flinging herself into the back of the car, she didn't say a word, instead giving me a "move along" gesture with her fingers as if she was shooing a fly. When I sat there for a moment to peer in the *Thomas Guide* in search of the route to her house, she finally deigned to speak, grunting, "Just go." So I started driving and within moments she picked up the car phone. *Shit.* I cleared my throat tentatively. "Um, Ms. Davidovich, you aren't actually supposed to use the phone." I certainly didn't want to get into a confrontation with my first client, but I did want to follow the rules. She completely ignored me, putting the phone to her ear.

"Hello, Mother," she said, rolling the "l" in "hello" in an affected way. And who other than gay men, the British, and especially British gay men still used the word "mother" that way? I was temporarily thrown off my task of getting her off the phone while I tried to figure out the accent. Ever since *Charlie's Angels.* It had always been a dream of mine to work as a private eye. I imagined that determining the origin of accents was a big part of that job, so this would be perfect practice. I detected what I thought to be a Russian overtone, muted by a slight Montreal dialect, with subtle tones of German spy. "Mooother, I doubt I'll be on time for lunch," she muttered into the phone. "The girl doesn't even know where she's going." My conclusion: she was from somewhere extremely annoying.

While she talked away, I stewed; I'd been told if the phone was used when it wasn't authorized, the driver was responsible for the cost, and so far I'd cleared only thirteen dollars for the first hour of the ride. I waited until Lolita had me stop at a 7-Eleven and I called in to dispatch: "Um, I've got Lolita Davidovich in my car and she's been on the phone and I tried to tell her she's not authorized but, well, am I going to have to pay for it?"

"If you want to keep your job you do" was the fuzzy reply from my radio just as Lolita slid back into the car, scooped the phone back up, and started punching buttons. I tried to politely tell her again that she wasn't cleared for the phone but maybe I didn't say it loud enough, because she didn't even make eye contact. It was a dilemma, because if I pushed it, I'd probably get no tip, and if I was going to have to cover the charges, I would definitely need more money than my base wage. I decided to keep my mouth shut and let her yap on and on, praying she wasn't using the minutes to

call Germany. *Please keep it to this continent,* I pleaded
silently. Didn't really matter; she completely stiffed me.
And that's when I started getting slightly worried that
depending on famous people to make my rent might
not be the gold mine I'd hoped for.

Dispatch instructed me to turn around and head
back to LAX to await my next client. There was a
taxi/limo lot where the drivers stationed themselves
while they waited. It was mostly older foreign men
who stood next to their cars talking in clusters of three
or four, chain-smoking stinky cigarettes until they got
their call, jumped back in, and sped off like a police
car to an emergency. My wait lasted for seven hours. I
watched with rising panic as other limo drivers from
my company with seniority barely parked for five minutes before pulling back out to go fetch another client.
Over the radio I heard Big Al get assigned to pick
up Kelly Preston. He waved as he zoomed past my
parked town car on his way to International Arrivals.
Ortiz got David Crosby and I continued to alternate
between dozing and reading chapters of *Waiting to
Exhale,* which I'd been forced to buy at the airport gift
shop for full price because I hadn't known there'd be
this much unpaid downtime.

When I dragged myself in the door that night at

eleven p.m., having cleared only the twenty-six dollars from driving Lolita Davido*bitch,* I wanted nothing more than to eat leftover Chinese food and go straight to bed. But as I swung open my bedroom door, the last thing I saw was flying paws before I was knocked on my ass. By the time I struggled to my feet I saw it: a huge mountain of foam debris next to what had until recently been my Serta Perfect Sleeper mattress but was now merely a rectangle with a giant spring-filled crater in the middle. The plush pillow-top pad had been clawed apart and was strewn all over the room. *"Goddamn it, Georgia!"* I screamed furiously through clenched teeth. I had few luxuries in life as it was. This wasn't the first expensive item she'd damaged, but this went well beyond gnawing through a Kenneth Cole lace-up leather boot I'd bought on sale at Macy's or tearing a hole in the cover of the bean bag chair, allowing twelve cubic feet of Styrofoam filler particles to blanket our living room carpet. I had half a mind to whack her with the other lace-up boot—the one that was still intact and sitting on my floor as if it hadn't given up hope that its mate might someday return from the sea or a Macy's outlet sale.

Georgia looked at me so sadly. How could I be mad? I'd been a bad mommy, leaving her home for fourteen hours straight with nothing but a single walk from my neighbor. I'd have to do better. I had a family now . . . responsibilities. But I'd need to keep this job for a while longer, if for no other reason than to be able to buy a new goddamn mattress.

I really should've known better than to have gotten even the tiniest bit excited about picking up Justine Bateman, but I couldn't help myself—I'd grown up with Mallory and the rest of the Keatons! I sang, "What would we do, baby, without us, what would we dooo, baby, without us . . . sha la la la," all the way to the airport pickup, giddy with anticipation of a possible friendship and some Meredith Baxter Birney dirt, and hopeful that today would be the day this job turned around.

I'd waited at her gate almost two hours, holding my sign with her name on it to alert her that I was her driver. I was even wearing the cap. The moment Justine and her sister approached me, I noticed their carry-ons were the size of fertilizer sacks. I reasoned that being America's lovable sitcom sister must result in some real leeway at check-in. Without a word, she and her sister pushed the giant bags into my hands and let me teeter along with them down the length of the terminal past all the gates while they giggled about their trip. At baggage claim skis and giant gear bags added to the load.

Even once in the car they didn't utter a word to me the entire way to Studio City until Justine finally said, "Pull in here so we can grab a quick bite." Hardly the lively conversation between new best gal pals that I'd envisioned. And now here I was, forty minutes later, waiting, fuming, and starving. *I bet she doesn't even tip me,* I thought.

So maybe I was mad, or maybe I was just really tired, but when I dropped Justine and her sister at their house, dragged their luggage to the doorstep, thanked them for the ten-dollar tip, and got back behind the wheel, I didn't notice that I'd gotten too close to the massive ornamental stone along the side of the driveway. But I did notice when the entire underside of the bumper and rear panel scraped against it, making a noise so loud I was sure the whole neighborhood heard it. The end-of-day instructions were to take the car in for a wash and fill it with gas so that it would be ready for the early run the next day. *Screw it,* I thought as I wheeled toward the on-ramp. *What's the point now?* So I just drove back to dispatch; parked the car; waved to Barbara, who was reloading water and candy in her limo's cab; and got in my own car and drove home. I knew then I would never see the sweater she would have knitted for Georgia. It was okay, I had a feeling it wouldn't have been at all flattering.

That night I was home early, and I cuddled with my neurotic dog while we watched our favorite, *Unsolved Mysteries*. It was a really nice moment for us, and I briefly considered taking some time off to be with Georgia. But I knew I would need to get back to work soon and I'd just never really seen myself as the stay-at-home-mom type. As much as I was devoted to Georgia, I was a career woman, and I needed to mix it up with the outside world and just be around other humans. But whatever job I got, it wouldn't be with a limo company again, because it was pretty certain by the next day I'd no longer have a spotless driving record.

How I Stopped Worrying and Learned to Love the Bomb

People love to hear about what it's like to bomb as a stand-up comic. And I fully get why. It's always fascinating to hear tales of people living through tragic near-death experiences. No one wants to hear about the time you accidentally hit the accelerator instead of the brakes and rolled through a red light, and thank God no one was coming from the opposite direction, or you could've died! No, they want to hear about the out-of-control Mack truck that slammed into you doing eighty on the freeway, causing a nine-car pileup and resulting in your tracheotomy scar and kidney loss.

Luckily for me, I've had a million bombing experiences.

My friend Lisa Sundstedt has a joke that goes, "People often say to me, 'Oh my God, Lisa, I can't believe you do stand-up comedy, that's so scary. Do you ever bomb?' And I say, 'Of course! That's the nature of comedy; sometimes I'm super funny, and sometimes the audience sucks.'" I love this joke because it's true; comedy is scary and if you're going to survive it, you can't always take it personally.

For instance: the first time I ever bombed, I mean seriously bombed, as a stand-up comedian on television was on a show for an upstart cable network, which turned out, unbeknownst to me, to be a no-win situation. I was chosen for the show right after performing my "single girl sleeps around in the city"–type act, chatting about my vagina while an enthusiastic crowd of twenty ate dim sum.

The night before the show, which was filmed in front of a huge audience at a well-known comedy club, all of the comedians gathered for a tech rehearsal to receive our final instructions from the producer. The wardrobe speech, which is usually just "no red, white, or loud patterns," was different this time: "Ladies, keep it conservative. No excessive cleavage or overly sexy attire." And then he warned us about our material. "As for your act, absolutely no foul language or inappropriate subject matter." *Inappropriate for what?* I wondered. In stand-up most comics start with inappropriate as a base and within minutes work their way to downright tasteless. Not really knowing what he meant but not wanting to ask and look unprofessional, I figured I'd just do my normal act, minus the F-word. That seemed like it would be a more than adequate adjustment.

The next night, sitting in the hair and makeup chair, I got the first inkling I might have a problem. "I felt so bad about that other girl who went up in the last taping," the hairstylist said to the woman applying my blush with a sponge.

"What do you mean?" I asked. This was information I needed to have.

"It didn't go very well and she was in tears afterward," Hair said.

"Totally streaked her mascara," Makeup added.

Wow. People don't cry after TV tapings; people eat baby carrots in the greenroom while drinking free wine and schmoozing other people's agents. What kind of craziness was afoot?

"Was she funny?" I asked. I needed to make sense of this because it was rare to bomb on television, considering the audience assumes the comedian is funny or they wouldn't be on TV in the first place. TV tapings are supposed to be like swimming in the shallow end of the pool with a floatie vest and water wings; they're supposed to be safe. And now I was worried.

"I don't think she was spreading a very positive message," Makeup said.

"Sweet girl. Her jokes just weren't right for a born-again Christian comedy show," Hair said. *Christian? Oh Jesus Christ this was bad!* I thought.

"But she looked great!" Hair and Makeup cracked themselves up. Just like that my wading pool became a shark tank and I knew I was probably going to bomb.

It was bad. Right from the get-go, the crowd was having none of me. In fact, during one joke about leaving earrings at a guy's house to make sure he'd call again, I could see a woman in the audience actually shake her head disapprovingly at me, as if to say, "You definitely won't be going to heaven." My best jokes were met with dead silence and a few shocked intakes of air. You'd have thought I was saying "Jesus can suck it" the way the audience was reacting—or not react-

ing, as was the case. But I was forced to fake a smile
and pretend everything was fine to the huge room of
people and five television cameras that knew better.
The worst part was seeing those cameras and knowing
there would be a record of this night—like a sex tape,
only with fewer laughs.

Dying onstage is terrifying. It's not the actual
performing that's so scary; it's the worry that it won't
go well. I've never been scared shitless that I might
get huge laughs. I've never wished I'd taken a Xanax
before walking onstage because I was anxious people
would find me *too* funny, that they would fall into
hysterics after every joke, requiring me to slow down
and have a sip of water while I allowed them to catch
their breath. I've never felt sick with concern that I
simply wouldn't have *time* to high-five everyone in
the crowd after I killed. What I fear is the void, the
silence, which is the opposite of acceptance. When I
stand naked onstage with just my thoughts and expressions, I'm petrified I might be exposing myself as
a fraud, or worse, a fool for believing that I might have
something special. This is why no one respects a prop
act. Those people aren't naked; they have a steamer
trunk full of stupidity to put between themselves and
the crowd.

After my performance in the born-again show, four people told me they'd pray for me. At least they were polite.

The worst response I ever got bombing was a New Year's Eve gig in Fresno, California. The situation had two huge things going against it right off the bat: New Year's Eve and Fresno. But having been doing stand-up for only a couple of years, I hadn't had nearly enough experience to know that this was a losing combo. And I certainly didn't have the skill or confidence to overcome the circumstances. But even if I'd known what was in store, I still wouldn't have turned down a paying gig, not when it could lead to more paying gigs, and not considering some of the places where I'd gratefully performed for free.

I'd paid my dues performing in the early days for no pay on lineups of more than twenty comics at coffee shops, bookstores, bars, and bowling alleys. I screamed my act at a county fair to the leftover fans of a heavy metal band who were too drunk to get up and leave when the band was done. I once performed in a sports bar where I thought I was killing; the audience was whooping it up and cheering for me, though sometimes not *quite* at the right spots. Finally I looked over my shoulder to the left of the bar and sure enough, the Lakers game was showing. And it was having a great show! I'd said yes to gigs at rehabs and shelters. I'd driven an hour to a piano bar once to do an open mic night and the only person there was the piano player. Luckily he was a good laugher.

Driving the three hours to Fresno, I had mixed feelings. I felt lucky to get the gig but I was worried about the pressure of filling thirty minutes. I really had only about ten truly solid minutes, fifteen to twenty if I threw in every joke I'd ever written and twenty-five if I did a little crowd work. I spent part of the drive giving myself a Stuart Smalley–type pep talk in the rearview mirror: "You're good enough, you're funny enough, and god*damn* it, people like you!" And then I tried to come up with more jokes.

The venue was a restaurant, which apparently was a ghost town during the week, but Thursday through Sunday it came alive with two-dollar well drinks and comedy. In honor of New Year's Eve, they were going all-out, charging seventy-five bucks a head for a plate of grilled salmon, a baked potato, one small pat of butter, a sprig of parsley, a glass of four-dollar champagne, and the main attraction: a comedy show—with comedians from Los Angeles!

The hundred-and-fifty-dollars-a-couple admission price made me a nervous wreck. Even though I told myself that there were three comics on the show—it wasn't all on me to set the tone for the crowd's entire year to come—it created a lot of pressure to be funny. I paced the back of the room, trying to figure ways to get out of it. Maybe a migraine? I did feel like I might have the beginnings of one.

Unlike a lot of comics, I'd never been one of those people who get excited to go onstage. I'd never felt like "Let me at 'em, wait till they see this! Why doesn't this hack who's onstage right now hurry up and finish so I can get up there!" Never. Try as I might, I could never think of stand-up as enjoyable. Of course, if I think about it, this attitude isn't just about stand-up; I feel this way about a lot of things: writing, cleaning, and sex—I rarely look forward to the actual work involved but I'm usually pleased with the end result. And, come to think of it, I've used a migraine as an excuse to get out of all three. But this was worse: looking at the crowd of expectant audience members, all the time I'd spent on self-affirmations earlier in the car went right out the window. I felt wracked with fear, wondering why the hell I wanted to do this for a living. Why would I possibly put myself in a position like this? What had I been thinking?

Like many other times before going out onstage, I promised myself that if I just got through this night, I'd quit doing stand-up and really do something positive with my life, like use my earnings to buy a small house in Somalia and run an orphanage for special-needs children whose parents had either abandoned them or didn't have the means to care for them. I figured those kids could use a few laughs and would probably be a pretty receptive audience. It would be a win-win.

Now, normally, after all that freaking out, once I got my first big laugh, my jangling nerves would become background music and my inner performer would take control. But not this time. My first joke got nothing. My second joke got nothing. And due to the pressurized situation I'd helped create for myself, I imploded. Bailing on an entire chunk of material, I went straight for a tried-and-true joke and was met with dead silence. Well, that was just unheard of. (Unless the audience is born-again Christians. But this was Fresno; if you're stuck living in Fresno, you probably think there is no God.) Not knowing what else to do, I continued my act. But it had been less than three minutes and I'd already burned through ten minutes of material. And worse still, the audience was getting pissed.

"Where are you from?" I asked a couple sitting in the front row.

"Fresno," the guy answered, bored.

"Oh. I'm sorry," I said.

"Why? Fresno's a great place," the woman shouted back, reminding me that it's never a good idea to bait the audience when things aren't going well.

I could hear a woman a few rows back in an IT AIN'T GONNA LICK ITSELF T-shirt whispering loudly to her friend. Without thinking I said, "Hey, thanks for dressing up for New Year's," and she yelled back, "You suck!" The audience howled. Someone else yelled, "Get some jokes. You're not funny."

I'd never in all my time doing stand-up inspired anger in a crowd. Sure, I'd had my fair share of harmless heckling, but never just people yelling mean shit out at me. I didn't know what to do and I was in danger of bursting into tears. Nine times out of ten, crying will not inspire laughs, so I said, "Thank you, good night," and got the hell off the stage. When I checked my watch, I'd been onstage for six minutes. Somehow I doubted I'd be getting paid. Since there was no greenroom for the comedians to hang out in, I was forced to remain in the kitchen crying and eating dinner rolls dipped in ranch dressing until the show was finally over and the audience left. It was definitely a low point.

You'd think by how horrifying I've found it is to bomb that I would never set out to purposely do poorly, but there was a situation where I did just that. My friend Dino and I had a two-night gig at a run-down comedy club in Palm Springs, where we were making the cool sum of fifty dollars a night—each, baby, each! Okay, it wasn't a lot of money, but since Dino and I were good friends who really got a kick out of each other, we figured we'd have a good time making the two-hour trek each way, working on jokes, and watching each other's act. Plus, we were going to be put up in a condominium where we could hang out all day by the pool—what was not to like? We were to be the middle acts, each performing for fifteen minutes before the headliner took the stage for forty-five minutes after us.

The trouble started with the accommodations. Now, no comedians are ever expecting a five-star resort when they're playing a fifty-dollar gig, but when we walked into the condominium where the comics were

put up week after week, we were appalled: trash was everywhere, on every surface—gross trash. On the coffee
table was a petrified McDonald's meal. When I poked
it with a pen, it fell apart. You'd think with the money
the booker was saving by barely paying his talent, he'd
have hired someone to clean once a year. When I went
into the bedroom, it was worse. The bedsheets had
pubes on them! I felt bile rise in my stomach but I
didn't want to puke because I was scared of getting
Ebola from leaning over the toilet. We couldn't afford
a hotel, but it seemed unthinkable to stay where we
were. Before we could come up with an alternative,
the phone rang. I put my T-shirt over the receiver and
picked it up, being careful to hold the mouthpiece
as far from my mouth as possible. It was Paulie, the
booker, whose voice sounded like he'd smoked eighty
cigarettes a day every day since he was in diapers.

"Listen," he said, breaking right away to hack up
a lung. "We only have three reservations for the show
tonight, so I'm canceling it." I could barely understand
him, as he'd preemptively had his voice box surgically
removed. "See you tomorrow night."

"Well, are we still getting paid?" I heard him pull
air through his nose and into his throat, making a horrific sound like a phlegm avalanche.

"Half." And then he just hung up. Dino and I were furious, but rather than get back in our car and hightail it home to LA, we decided our best course of action would be to go get a beer or two and regroup. And that's where we came up with the idea to give the worst show of our lives. It was a beautiful plan in its simplicity. Maybe we couldn't get Paulie to pay us for driving two hours each way to perform at his hovel of a club, and maybe we couldn't control the disgusting living conditions at his poor excuse for a condo, but we could control the quality of the product we delivered. And we figured he should get what he paid for. We were going to bomb on purpose, and just the thought of it sent us into evil hysterics.

That night we spread towels out on the two couches in the living room and plotted our upcoming show's demise. I would go on first and do all setups to my jokes with no punch lines. In addition I would try to seem even more nervous than usual just to make the audience uncomfortable. Dino would bring his guitar onstage with him but never play it. We thought it would be particularly discomfiting to the crowd if every time it seemed like Dino was about to play, he'd get sidetracked and forget. Even more importantly, he was going to repeat jokes over and over as if he'd just lost track of where he was. The whole strategy seemed genius, and for one of the first times ever I was genuinely excited to take the stage.

The plan hit a snag almost immediately. Despite the fact that the night before had been a bust audience-wise, the place was packed and the crowd was in a great mood. When I opened my set by announcing that I hadn't showered because the condo was too disgusting, the audience cracked up. I tried to explain in terms as non-funny as possible how gross our living conditions were but the audience continued chuckling, so I moved out of improvise mode straight into my success-proof material. "Do you ever notice how soap operas will change the actor that plays an important character with a different actor and no one will ever mention it?" Big laugh. This made *me* laugh because it was so stupid, which made them laugh even harder. I looked at Dino and shrugged my shoulders. "Sorry, Dino," I said right to him. "I don't know what their problem is. This is not funny stuff."

I went in hard for another attempt: "Sex in a dream is always good. You can't have bad sex in a dream." Dino dragged an ashtray across a table in an attempt to mask even a hint of a funny tone. Huge laugh. "No, seriously, let me explain: I haven't said anything funny yet." But their laughter was contagious and now *I* couldn't stop laughing. I felt like I was stoned. I had to turn it around! But I couldn't; the more setups I tried the bigger the laughs became, until I gave up. I had longed for a "you suck." I would've relished an uncomfortable moment but the audience could sense my confidence and they refused to dislike me.

Dino suffered the same fate. He opened his set with the joke that he planned on retelling: "I had mice in my house and I thought I'd get an unconventional means to kill them. I'd get a cat to kill them. But the cat was way too vicious. He didn't kill them, he'd rape them and leave them for dead. I got back at him though; I drove him insane. I bought a record of a can opener opening over and over again." Unfortunately the audience loved the joke so much it ruined any chance of him not seeming funny. Every time he started to retell it, the audience cheered him on. By the time he started the joke for the fourth time, I was laughing so hard I felt like I might need medical attention. The same went for Dino and his plan to not ever actually play his guitar. He'd pick it up to play it and then put it back down, and the audience would howl because they thought it was part of the act.

After the show, Paulie came over with our check.

"Guys, the audience loved you. I'm still not going to be able to pay you for all of last night, but I want you to come back and coheadline." Of course we agreed, because a gig's a gig. Driving home, Dino and I had to agree that it was the best we'd ever bombed in our careers.

California Fruit

It was approximately one p.m. when my manager Todd called me out of the blue all excited. A California Fruit campaign was casting a national commercial and he'd pulled some strings and gotten them to squeeze me in for an audition. "How soon can you be in Santa Monica?" he asked. The main problem was I was currently sitting in a stuffy office in the San Fernando Valley on my first day of a temp job at a law firm. This was a serious assignment; it involved pantyhose. I was busily typing sixty address labels into a computer, address labels that would need to be affixed to sixty packages, packages that would need to be in a FedEx office by five o'clock.

It was now a little into the lunch hour and all I'd eaten was what I scavenged from the desk of the chick I was replacing. I'd turned up a couple of sleeves of store-brand saltines that had lost the timeless battle between humidity and cracker, as well as two shiny Percocets winking at me from a prescription bottle. They were likely from some recent dental work: a "DDS" came after the prescribing doctor's name, and that's the kind of detail a self-taught private eye learns to pick up. I'd gone ahead and swallowed one with the last of my coffee. Hey, she may have had a toothache but I was in a lot of psychic pain, and to be honest I was pretty proud of myself for even leaving her one. But now that I was wrestling with the sudden shock of an unplanned commercial audition, I went ahead and took the other one, too. She'd understand that it was best for us both, because the poster behind her desk stressed the merits of teamwork.

I never did well on acting auditions, which wasn't too surprising because I wasn't a good actress. However, unlike 90 percent of the actresses in Hollywood, I could admit that to myself, and, without much prod-ding, to the casting directors, who probably didn't need to be told. I preferred to remain honest about these things. That way, there were no unmet expectations and no one got disappointed. Acting is just one of the many areas in which I have zero ability. There's also

singing, dancing, calligraphy, tying a scarf, trouble-
shooting, controlling my emotions, celebrity impres-
sions, believable foreign accents, sketching, crafts of
any kind, and 69, which I always felt was like trying
to pat your head and rub your stomach at the same
time—another thing I wasn't good at. The list could
really go on and on since I'm finding new ones all the
time. Lack of skills in these areas has never caused me
too much trouble, but not being able to act has caused
endless embarrassment.

"Bring a headshot," my manager was saying, "and
put on some makeup." What the hell? Could he see me
through the phone? "And this is critical—*be positive.*
You really need to book something. It's time." Not *It's
your time.* Just *It's time.* Subtle difference, but it felt a
little threatening.

While I was busy being honest with myself, my
manager was living in a fantasyland regarding my abilities. He thought I just hadn't had the right audition
yet and that I needed new headshots. I'd always hated
the way I looked in photographs because I had an
excessively gummy smile, and smiling on purpose only
exacerbated the problem. I'd practiced endlessly, trying
by feel to detect when my lips had revealed my teeth
but hadn't slipped up so high that I was showing the

full Molly Ringwald. But this was much easier said than done. It seemed ridiculous to pay a fancy photographer five hundred dollars just so I could hate the way I looked under extra lighting, so I'd waited until I really needed a headshot, any headshot, and then paid a guy fifty bucks to snap some photos using his garage door as a backdrop. The results sort of resembled a mug shot with lip gloss, and between my hair and eyebrows, I appeared to suddenly have become Hispanic. I'd used the bad picture once, and given the negative response, the remaining two hundred and ninety nine remained in the trunk of my Buick waiting for the call to come for a Latina-gang-leader-with-big-gums type. Subsequent attempts weren't much better. I suppose this could have been part of the reason for my constant commercial audition failures. Well, that and my complete inability to improv.

"Todd, I don't think I can go because I'm at a job," I said as quietly into the phone as I could, not that it mattered since most people were at lunch.

"You're on an acting job and you didn't tell me? What is it?"

"No. It's a *job* job. Law firm. It's my first day."

"You get a lunch break, don't you?" my manager said, pushing back.

"Well, I guess technically, but I have to get this stuff ready for FedEx."

"Just go right now. Go. Go. Go. I'm counting on you. You'll be able to get right back to file legal briefs or whatever you're doing."

"Are you sending anyone else out for this?" I asked, hoping he had a fallback plan.

"Yeah, three girls." By three, I knew he meant four, including Carol. She was my manager's wife and was even less of an actress than I was. But she had access to the breakdowns—the top-secret lists of casting calls from all the shows that are looking to cast—from her husband's office and regularly used a yellow highlighter to make it clear to him which auditions she expected to go on. Needless to say, I saw her at almost every one. "But you're perfect for this. You just need to believe."

It was 1:20 p.m. when I turned up the freeway on-ramp. Traffic from the Valley to Santa Monica was especially brutal around the lunch hour, and no matter how many shortcuts a person knew (and I knew a few—hell, I'd driven a limo for weeks!), it was tough to avoid the 405. And if you got stuck on the 405 you weren't getting anywhere in under an hour.

As I sat there in bumper-to-bumper traffic, the scenario was ripe for me to obsess about where my life had veered so far off the tracks. The only reason I agreed to the audition was because I felt I was dangerously close to getting dropped by my manager. I was shocked he hadn't taken me off his roster yet, considering I'd never booked an acting job the entire time he'd been representing me. I knew I probably shouldn't be going on any sort of formal auditions, given my lack of talent. But the alternatives as a nonacting stand-up comedian were limited: I could go on the road, touring the country as a middle act, telling jokes in Toledo in hopes of one day being the headliner, or I could stay in Los Angeles, do a little stand-up here and there, and be forced to admit to myself that my days of filing and labeling were no longer "temp." I guess I wasn't quite ready to give up my lifelong dream of doing very little in exchange for adulation, an overinflated ego, and, of course, a sweet chunk of money.

Discovering that I didn't possess a shred of acting ability had taken me by surprise. I'd been under the impression that I'd be a natural. It certainly didn't seem that hard. After all, I'd been the hit of the Jewish Community Center's production of *The Wizard of Oz* when I was seven. I'd landed the coveted role of Dorothy and *killed* it. (The zaidies and bubbies were all up in my business for weeks.) And since doing stand-up, I'd gotten a lot of opportunities, I just wasn't able to turn the opportunities into anything.

My problem wasn't lack of effort. At Todd's strong suggestion, I'd signed up for expensive acting classes and had actually gone for a few months, a few of the most painful months of my life. In my very first class, I was forced to lie on the floor and pretend to be a piece of bacon sizzling in a pan. Any endeavor that begins with pan work is not headed in a good direction. It was humiliating and I'd felt like an asshole, and yet, I gave my bacon debut all I had. I imagined I must've looked like I was having a grand mal seizure with all my effort, but the teacher called me out for a lackluster sizzle.

Throughout the session, it was clear my problem was that I had a hard time letting go. I was inhibited. In scenes my voice always came out sounding more like C-3PO than the natural actress I heard in my head. No matter how many relaxation exercises I did in class, my performance always came across as stiff and reserved. When I was attempting a scene with a partner, I tried every Method acting trick to get lost in the world. I would ask myself, "What would I do if I were in these circumstances? How would I behave?" But my answer to myself would always be, "How do I know? I'm not in these circumstances. I'm in acting class looking like a dumb-ass." And no matter how much I practiced, I could never make my eyes water by *feeling* myself peeling an onion, but I could make myself crave a burger.

And so, in and out of class, I was a poor excuse for an actress. After the few auditions I'd been on, the feedback to Todd always was "Too wooden. Too green. She needs to take a class. And lose weight." Always with the losing weight. Inevitably, I'd cry over the discouraging news, then eat to blot out those feelings.

But if theatrical auditions were a low point, commercial auditions were my Mariana Trench.

At a little after two p.m., I finally pulled into the parking lot for the commercial casting office, only a few short hours before I needed to be at FedEx. I'm not sure of the *exact* time since it wasn't the most excruciating detail of the afternoon's trauma, but I do know I was already a bit tense. The waiting area was bursting with activity as I walked through the door. The first thing I expected to see as I swung past the front desk of a casting call was the usual group of LA actresses: impeccably made up; dressed in faded 501 jeans, black bodysuits, and black cowboy boots; and each one underweighing me by a good fifteen pounds. But now, I was confronted instead with what looked like a room full of Edie McClurg impersonators—

character actresses with frizzy hair and bold eye shadow colors applied like Mimi from *The Drew Carey Show* to accentuate wackiness! I was by far the youngest person in the room and, judging from the competition, completely wrong for this job.

At least for once I was the thinnest person in the room.

How could Todd have thought I was perfect for this job? I figured I should call him.

"Todd, I think they're looking for a very specific type here and it's not me. This is going to be a waste of time."

"It's never a waste to get face time with big casting directors. If you think they are looking for something else, get in there and change their minds! Gotta run, lunch just got here."

At 2:30, the person in charge of casting came out to give everyone our instructions for the interview. "First of all," he said, and then took a dramatic pause, "we're all going to have *a lot* of fun in there today. This commercial is for the California Fruit Board and we're excited and honored to have Mr. Adam Arkin directing it." Looking like he was about to disclose the details of the Manhattan Project, he continued. "I think you will all find the creative concept pretty exciting: You are playing a bored, lonely housewife who gets a taste of a ripe juicy green grape. The flavor of this California grape is so decadent that you lapse into a sensual daydream that a young, shirtless Adonis is feeding you grapes. Getting attention from this young hottie naturally sends you into a fit of sexual pleasure. Any questions?"

Yeah, I had few. For one: *What the fuck?*

"This sounds like you're looking for us to do a fake orgasm kind of thing," said one of the Edies as if it were her absolute favorite thing to do in a public setting.

"Yes. That's the bit." Now I was getting enormously tense. I'm not particularly comfortable having a *real* orgasm in the privacy of my own bedroom, and now I was going to have to fake one in a room full of people, including the dude from *Chicago Hope*? I raised my hand very slightly.

"Hi, sorry, I have a question: Are there sides?"

"There's a loose script, but please feel free to improvise." That's basically the last thing I wanted to hear at an audition. Well, next to hearing the audition entailed faking an orgasm, that is. Commercial casting people are obsessed with an actor's ability to improvise, but I couldn't stand having to improvise. I'd once accidentally joined an improv group before

I ever tried stand-up because I thought it would help me get used to being onstage. The problem was these people thought the height of hilarity was doing any character with an Irish brogue, as a crazy homeless bum, as someone from another planet who speaks only alien, or a combination of all three. I preferred to just be myself and not have to make anything up on the spot if at all possible. Thus, I was not included in many scenes, which was fine with me. The only thing I enjoy less than doing improv is attending an improv performance. It's the comedy equivalent of jamming. I'd rather smooth out my eyeball with a Ped Egg than sit through an evening of people onstage yelling out, "Can I have a suggestion for a household object?" and "I need a situation that a man and woman would be fighting about." If it's up to me, the audience member, to come up with all the scene suggestions, then I'm working way too hard.

I took a glance around the room to see who was with me on this whole nightmare, but if anyone was unhappy they sure weren't showing it. Most of them looked like faking an orgasm as the culmination to a scene they have to make up as they go along was just par for Tuesday. Clearly, Adam Arkin couldn't have known what was in store for him in this murderers' row.

I thought of making a beeline for the door, but as I war-gamed out the inevitable call to Manager Todd in my head, each scenario ended with his dropping me as a client. I sat down. One of the Edies was gnawing off her nails and humming quietly in the process. I wanted to throw up. It was a good thing I'd brought along a few of those generic saltines for sustenance, because now I needed them to calm my stomach.

It was now 2:45 and they were bringing the girls in one by one. My name was fairly far down the list. I checked the sheet for Carol, Todd's wife, but she'd never signed in, and I hadn't seen her. Either she'd hightailed it out of there when she found out the concept for this commercial, or Todd had warned her ahead of time and she'd gone to a Miss Clairol call instead.

2:50 p.m.—I heard loud moaning from the audition room and I knew it was coming from a Midwestern, middle-aged, pear-shaped professional improviser named Dolly. I felt like I might hurl again, only now I was out of crackers. I'm not sure what was making me more ill: the mental image of Dolly having an orgasm, or the realization that she'd probably just booked this job.

3:00 p.m.—I'd now been gone from the law firm for two hours. If I left right now, I'd make it back in time to attach the labels and get to FedEx.

3:10—I was next. *Shit.*

3:17—The door opened and I found myself standing in a conference room facing a long table of suits; it was very similar to the audition scene in *Flashdance.* There were a camera, a cameraman, ad people, producers, and, as promised, Mr. Adam Arkin. I was ushered in front of the camera to slate, which is where you look straight at the camera and say your name, and Adam Arkin stepped over to shake my hand. He gave me a quick smile but made only the briefest eye contact, which I sort of understood; he probably didn't want to get too attached. We were about to share an extremely intimate moment and he was aware of the harsh reality of the business: after all was said and done there was a good chance I wouldn't be the one. Actually I had a better chance of winning the lottery, since winning the lottery didn't require talent.

Suddenly I realized what I was doing: self-sabotaging. I was there, wasn't I? Todd was right: I had to believe in myself or nothing would ever change. I was scrappy. Nothing had ever been just handed to me, and it probably wasn't going to start now. So if I wanted to book this job, I was going to have to jump right in and go for it! I needed to channel a little less Eeyore and a little more Tony Robbins if I wanted to be successful.

"Okay, hon. You're a lonely housewife who's unfulfilled, frazzled, giving all her energy to the kids day after day, year after year . . . you get the picture. And then Bradley's going to come in and give you some grapes. The grapes are so unbelievably juicy, they make you instantly imagine Bradley's your love slave." Bradley, wearing Dockers and a bored expression, got up from the conference table and stood right off to the side of the frame.

"Are there any actual grapes I could have?" I figured they might help me get into character and also, I was pretty hungry.

"No. California grapes aren't even in season right now. Pretend. You got it? You ready?"

Oh, I got it: I had to fake an orgasm in a room full of cameras, producers, the star of *Chicago Hope,* and now some guy in Dockers named Bradley. I was ten years too young and I was about to go for it.

3:20—I attempted to say a few lines and then fake an orgasm. It came off as sexy as you'd expect: like C-3PO saying a few lines and then C-3PO blowing a fuse.

3:22—No one made eye contact or even said, "Thank you for coming in," which normally is the kiss of death, but I'd have taken it now.

3:32—I pulled onto the on-ramp for the 405 north to take me back to the Valley. I'd been gone from the law firm for over two hours but I'd have been gone for three by the time I got back. FedEx by five was looking bleak.

I shouldn't have gone to the audition. Now I would most likely miss the cutoff for FedEx and possibly lose this temp job because of it.

I merged onto the 101 west and started looking for my exit in order to veer right off the freeway and back to work, my safety net. I got into the "exit only" right lane and slowed as the exit came up to meet me. Miraculously I pulled back into the law firm parking lot at 4:20, slipping back into my desk chair unnoticed at 4:25. I finished printing out my address labels as quickly as possible. If I hurried I'd actually make it. Some of the other women in the office were giving me dirty looks; taking a three-hour lunch break wasn't exactly done, at least not by professionals—or by people who made a concerted effort not to get fired. *Why did I put myself in this position?* I asked myself. But I knew why; I needed acting to save me from the alternative: this being my desk permanently, wearing control-top pantyhose every day, driving a Cabriolet, and getting angry at people for eating the pasta salad I'd left in the refrigerator in a Tupperware container with my name on it.

When I got back from FedEx Todd called. "So, they're going a different way on the California Fruit Board campaign. But good news: Adam Arkin said he thinks you could stand to gain a few pounds. Also, I got you Listerine for tomorrow morning."

So screw it; even if I wasn't good at it I needed the opportunities, I needed the hope. And what *if* I couldn't fake an orgasm in a room full of people? Personally, I didn't see why anyone needed a *When Harry Met Sally* scene to sell grapes. Why did we have to bring sex into it? If I'd written that commercial I would have gone a different way too. And let's face it, you didn't need to be Meryl fucking Streep to sell Listerine either; if they were smart it would just require looking into the camera and feigning sincerity and fresh breath. Why couldn't I sell grapes this way?

I had one more thing to do before I left for the day: I needed to let my boss know I wouldn't be in until at least ten a.m. Although, knowing traffic, more likely eleven—hey, it was the professional thing to do.

The Big Date

The year was 1995, and I was flat broke and drink-ing heavily in Barney's Beanery, a pub in West Hollywood frequented by showbiz types, fans of fancy beer from tiny breweries that turn out three cases a year, and people way too into billiards. I've never ap-preciated the allure of shooting pool. I feel strongly the game is mainly for people who can't muster the energy to go bowling but still want to enjoy a sport that offers steady access to all-you-can-eat wings. But since my friend Nina was buying me drinks to help soothe me after my latest in a string of restaurant firings, I wasn't in a position to veto her choice of venue. Nina and I were sitting at the one little round table we'd staked out in a sea of pool tables and I was enjoying my fourth exotic beer, some black beer from Brazil (whose label promised that it was brewed a way that preserved the rain forest), when I noticed Jasmine drinking at the bar.

At first I wasn't sure; after all, it had been about four years since I skipped out on appearing on *Studs*. For the record, I was still fairly confident about my decision in spite of a momentary crisis of faith when I saw my episode and José—my almost husband—was in fact somewhat hot. But when I noticed Jasmine staring at me like she knew me from somewhere but just couldn't quite place it, I realized it had to be her. Even though I was happy I didn't go on the show, I still sort of felt sheepish running into her. I'd second-guessed Jasmine's matchmaking abilities and convinced myself that she was interested only in making good TV by matching me up with a pirate and not in finding me the true love I felt should have awaited . . . on *Studs*. But maybe I'd underestimated her both personally and professionally; after all, she was a gainfully employed television producer, and I was an out-of-work waitress with no prospects. I jotted down *Work on being less self-important* on my mental to-do list and tried to come up with a life plan.

"I just can't get another waitress job," I said to Nina. "No one will hire me." I'd recently been fired from four waitressing jobs in the course of a month.

That had to be some sort of regional record. In calmer moments, I told myself this was God's way of telling me to stop waiting tables, but most of the time I remembered that I was fresh out of viable options to pay my rent, an extremely depressing thought, especially at twenty-eight. "I'm gonna have to work retail."

"Are you high? You can't work at the mall! Who does that? Nineteen-year-olds taking a year off from community college, and skeevy forty-year-old Radio Shack managers with degrees from DeVry." Nina clearly had issues with non-four-year institutes of higher learning.

"Well, what *am* I going to do? I've been fired from almost every waitressing job I've had. I have no references and I need money. My last source of income was a stand-up gig at the Natural Fudge Company and the pay was a free latte."

"Okay, let's think. What are you good at?" Nina worked at a theme park as a member of a doo-wop group, so I wasn't sure she was a great choice for a career counselor, but it was sweet of her to try.

"I'm a good drinker. I can drink whiskey straight without even flinching," I said, kind of proud.

"There you go. You could be a novelist."

"I've got ADD. I'd have to write short stories. Really short stories. Like ads."

"Or bumper stickers."

"Could be something there. I wonder how much venture capital I'd need to start my own bumper sticker business."

The problem with my solution of drowning my problems in fancy-boy beer was that now I needed to pee, and the only bathroom was located just beyond where Jasmine was perched at the bar. The space in front of her was tight and I'd physically need to squeeze past her to get to the restroom. I knew I would probably come face-to-face with Jasmine, and once I did she might figure out where we knew each other from and then I'd get a lecture about bailing on the rendezvous with my handpicked Stud, which was the last thing I needed in my current mind-set. If I didn't have to pee so badly, I'd have just as soon avoided the whole embarrassing situation.

I looked past Jasmine at the fluorescent clock above her head, as if I had an appointment or was timing my insulin injection, in an effort to see if this would be a good time to sneak by her, but she was looking right at me. *Shit. She knows,* I thought. But I had to go.

"Hey, excuse me, you look so familiar," Jasmine said predictably as I brushed past her. "Do I know you?" I thought for sure she'd made the connection and was plotting my demise, but was it possible she hadn't? After all, she probably met thousands of *Studs* hopefuls and I'd met only one dating show producer. And after all, wasn't I trying to be less self-important? Still, I was afraid to play the "where do we know each other" game for too long because I didn't want to help her figure it out.

"Hmm, I don't think so. But I get that a lot."

"Really?"

"Oh yeah. I guess I have that kind of look. A lot of people think I look like someone they know: a class-mate, neighbor, old coworker . . . you know." She was staring at me intensely, making me nervous.

"Have you ever been on a dating show?"

"On a dating show? No, God no. Why do you ask?"

"I was one of the producers on *Studs.*"

"You don't say?" She was so genuine that I couldn't tell if she was onto me or not. But if she wasn't calling me out, I certainly wasn't turning myself in. Not yet.

"I'm producing a new dating game show. I'd love to get you in as a contestant."

"Oh, that's so nice of you. Yeah, I, I, uh, have a boyfriend," I lied. "So, I probably shouldn't do some-thing like that because he's pretty jealous. But does the show need any writers?" My buzz made me brave. And what did I have to lose?

"I don't hire the segment producers," Jasmine said. I later found out that a segment producer is the game show equivalent of a writer. "But do you have a résumé that I could pass along to the supervising producer?" Jasmine was so fantastic I almost wished I'd gone on *Studs,* but, then again, if I'd gone on *Studs* I wouldn't be getting an opportunity to write! I made a mental note that if I got my first writing job—segment producer job, whatever, I'd definitely get her a card. And not a cheap card. I'd get her one of those Blue Mountain cards that talk about feelings, because once I had a real job, I'd be happy, and happy people are able to express sentimental thoughts without feeling like a pussy.

"A writing résumé? Of course," I lied for the second time in under a minute. As a waitress, résumés weren't really my calling card. "Let me just get your e-mail address and I'll get it over to you tomorrow!"

The next day I went next door to my neighbor Tate's apartment to ask him if he'd help me fabricate a passable "writer's" résumé on his computer. Even as late as 1995, scraping together enough disposable income to get a personal computer seemed as realistic as putting together the down payment for a personal zeppelin. Tate was a sweater-vesty sitcom writer whose apartment door faced mine in our rent-controlled building, and I often went to his place for a quick drink before I went out for the evening or to small gatherings with his writer friends. I hadn't actually seen him in a while because the month before, after having too much to drink, I slammed my finger in my front door and showed up at his apartment tipsy and sobbing at eleven o'clock at night. He gave me ice for my hand and set me up on his couch with an afghan while I cried. I hadn't been super clear on whether or not I accidentally ended up making out with him that night, since I was buzzed as well as in so much pain. Knowing myself, it seemed highly possible, but I didn't really want to come out and ask. I really hoped I hadn't because it would have been pretty awkward, plus he owned sweater vests and an afghan.

"Tate, I need your help," I said the next day, sitting on his couch. "I have a great opportunity to possibly work on this dating show, but I have to have a résumé."

"Do you have one?" Tate asked.

"Not for writing. I have an acting résumé, but I can't use that one. I don't think anyone at the show is going to care that I can do accents—which I can't, but I'm banking on the fact that no one's ever asked me to prove it. I figure if I ever book a job I could always hire a dialect coach or—"

"So you need to make one," Tate said, cutting me off.

"Isn't that kind of extreme?" I whined. I was sort of hoping he'd have a spare résumé that I could just borrow. Having to actually create a résumé from scratch seemed excessive. Shouldn't creative people just be able to recognize other creative people on sight and not feel the need to bring paperwork into it? People like that really should go with their instincts more and not get bogged down by specifics like "job history" and "prior arrests." I was just ahead of my time. I guess you can't force enlightenment.

"Have you worked on any television shows?" Tate asked, now looking intently at his computer screen.

"Not exactly."

"Not exactly?"

"No, but I have watched a ton of television. I consider myself an expert in the field."

"Yes, but *watching* TV doesn't really translate well on a résumé. Do you have any professional writing experience?" And that's when I pulled the ace out of my sleeve: Mr. Alan Thicke.

"It just so happens that I do. I used to work for Alan Thicke."

"The guy from *Growing Pains* Alan Thicke?"

"Exactamundo, Tate. I developed shows for him. That was my job. I was a development person. I've been to his house."

"Wow. That's crazy. Alan Thicke has a house?"

"Ha-ha. Very funny. Alan Thicke is about to acquire some prime real estate on my résumé, so pretend you're impressed." I was actually quite proud of the fact that I'd been handpicked out of a lineup of comedians one evening at the Improv on Melrose to possibly work for the guy I mostly knew as "Mike Seaver's dad." I'd gone to his place in Toluca Lake with my friend Cynthia whom I'd recruited to be my writing partner and material witness on the off chance there was trouble, and we'd tossed around ideas for scenes. Cynthia and I would be doing this work "on spec," which meant, in layman's terms, "for free," or to put it another way, Cynthia and I would provide jokes and dialogue for scripts that had not been bought by any network, studio, or production company in exchange for "expenses," a line on our résumés, and *an answering machine message from Alan Thicke that I played for my parents and every other person in my life who ever doubted that I'd make it in this town!* Mary Tyler Moore may have had her "throwing her hat in the air" moment, but I had "playing Alan's message." And now, those six weeks, years ago, of literally working for peanuts were finally paying off like I knew they would.

"So Alan Thicke. What else?"

"Aren't we good? Alan Thicke, am I right? Once they see that, don't they almost have to give me the job?" I'd always known that with that experience, I'd only need to be in the right place at the right time to unleash the Thicke credit and things would automatically fall into place.

"I think you're going to need something else." Well, this was disappointing. I supposed that Tate might know something I didn't, since he'd managed to get himself more than one job in the business. I wondered if it was at all possible to get a writing job based on life experience alone. Would grammar play an important role? It seemed that a lot of people in charge of hiring other people were sticklers for a diploma. In that moment I wished I hadn't quit college just 120 credits short of a degree.

But I could write jokes.

"My stand-up is full of jokes I've written. That's all I do is crank out jokes."

"Writing on a show is different. You have to work a lot of hours a day at a desk writing consistently funny lines." *Huh.* Granted, a lot of the jokes I wrote came at two in the morning in a Denny's, high on hash brown grease and the company of other funny people, or in my favorite place to come up with a joke: my shower. I supposed a dating show wouldn't allow me to write part-time from the shower even if I got a desk in there, but I figured I'd cross that bridge when I came to it. First I'd need to get the job.

I added what little else I could think of to round that sucker out and let Tate format it into some sort of "writer speak." Next I wrote a little letter of introduction to the supervising producer, detailing the close personal friendship I'd formed with Jasmine and her wish that I hold a job as a writer on his show. I sent it all off that very day and began the waiting game.

A couple of days later, I got *the* call. On the line was Mike, the supervising producer. Getting that call made me feel even more triumphant than I had the first time a guy called after I'd had sex with him for the first time—validating my belief that he was indeed into me. Mike had received my résumé and wanted to know whether or not I could come in for an interview. With no hesitation, I mentally put a down payment on a town house in Santa Monica. Nothing too fancy: two bedrooms, two baths, eat-in kitchen, high wood vaulted ceilings finished in glossy walnut, and parking. There would need to exist plenty of parking, because as a successful dating show segment producer, I figured I would be doing a lot of entertaining, and I certainly didn't want people driving up and down the streets of Santa Monica looking for parking.

My meeting was the following week, which left me plenty of time to obsess over what I should wear and to try to lose three pounds. Sure, being a dating show producer didn't require me to be skinny, but old habits die hard. I lived on one Lean Cuisine for a day and a half and then accidentally ate an entire roll of frozen cookie dough. By the following Monday, I was up a pound, but so what? Nothing could dampen my spirits.

The show was called *The Big Date,* and its offices were on Sunset and Vine in Hollywood, which I was fairly certain was right near the original location of Schwab's drugstore, where Lana Turner was discovered and turned into a movie star at sixteen. The irony of this wasn't lost on me. And as I grabbed a ticket from the automated parking stand, drove into the underground parking structure, and rode the elevator to the sixth floor, I was nervous but more hopeful than I'd been in a long time.

When I got home that day I was buzzing so hard I could have conducted electricity. I called my friend Nina immediately. "I interviewed for that job," I squealed as soon as she picked up. "And I think it went great!"

"Did you book it?" Nina asked. It was a joke we had where when one person said they'd had an audition, the other person asked if they'd booked it.

"I like my chances." And then I told about forty more people, since this was by far the biggest thing that had ever happened to me since my mother let me get my ears pierced at ten in an uncharacteristic moment of weakness.

Then I wrote some sample material for the show as requested by my soon-to-be new boss, Mike. And then I waited patiently for the phone to ring with a job offer.

"How long do you think it should take for them to get back to me?" I asked Tate the next day when the phone still hadn't rung. Somehow I'd felt the feeling in the meeting had been mutual and he'd want to call right away to keep the vibe flowing.

"There's really no telling."

"Well, what's the longest you've waited to find out about a job?"

"Sometimes they don't call at all." *Don't call at all?*

How do people live like that? It didn't seem like there were enough sedatives in the world to make all that unknowing tolerable.

After a few days, I called the office to follow up but no one took my call, so I left a message. I started to wonder if there were others. I didn't want to think that way, but I couldn't help but suspect that there might be some other possible segment producer applicants sniffing around. But then I talked myself down. Mike had taken me to the production lot to watch a run-through of the show. He wouldn't have taken me there unless he was serious about this thing, right? Had Mike escorted *other people* through lot security with just a nod? Had the guards nodded back at *them* like it was obvious they belonged, like they were born to be on a television production lot? Not likely. Then the thoughts were there again: Were they smarter than I was? Did they have more actual experience? Were they irritating Ivy League types? Because if that's what Mike wanted, some asshole Harvard grad straight off the *Lampoon,* it wasn't me. Of course, if that's what he wanted, he should have just told me up front and not gotten my hopes up. Because now, now I was emotionally invested.

Another two days went by. And with time, I mellowed. Even if I didn't get this job, now I had a real résumé, I told myself. And even just getting this taste of opportunity had sparked a hunger for more. I had the fire in my belly. I thought of going out and trolling other pool bars for familiar faces that might be working in television and craving some résumé. I wouldn't let this experience be for naught.

"Is this Stefanie? We'd like to offer you the job. How's $850 a week?" It was the executive producer. I died.

In that moment, my world changed. It didn't matter that I'd never gone to my senior prom. It didn't matter that I outweighed my pit bull by ninety-five pounds. It didn't matter that my last real boyfriend had abandoned me to move to Italy and was most likely screwing a new girl, a European girl. What mattered was I'd secured my first real job. Now I would have to do something I'd never done before, in any job or any relationship: keep it.

The phone rang again. Could it be more good news? It seemed likely; I was on a roll. It was my manager Todd. "I've got Odor-Eaters for you tomorrow at four. They want you to make up a song about smelly feet and bring it with you."

"Todd. I can't do it. I'm not going to be able to do any commercial auditions for a while."

"What? Why?" I did hate to let Todd down, especially since I still had yet to get a single callback. But it was better for both of us.

"I got a job as a segment producer! I'm a writer now."

And it was true.

If You Like It
Then You Should've
Put a Ring on It

It was while working out on the Santa Monica stairs that I decided it was high time I got my belly button pierced. I'd been doing the stairs for a few months and had trimmed my abs to at least a three-pack. I was looking hot. Maybe not by LA's brutal standards, but I was arguably a Boise ten. In fact, since my stomach had always been my non–problem area, I'd often wear a sports bra with a pair of baggy sweat shorts just so that people could check out all the nonsense I was bringing to the table in the tummy department. I kept the ass under wraps since that was definitely more of a work in progress.

I'd never been happy with the size of my ass since I was old enough to realize cellulite isn't a ticket to teen modeling. But my stomach was a different story. I'd been seeing a lot of belly rings and thought they looked pretty sexy. I'm definitely not easy that way. For people exercising in public, I have a long list of things I don't want to see. Like testicles, for one. If you're a dude in his forties or above, and you insist on wearing short shorts, and then you insist on climbing the steepest stairs directly in front of me, for God's sake put on some form of suspension garment that will shield my eyes from your sac. Another major eyesore? Visors. This may be the most unnecessary fashion accessory ever invented. If you ever find yourself shopping for a visor, why not just spring for a whole hat? Plus, there's the fact that anyone who would wear a visor is probably someone who would also wear jorts, the evil hybrid of jeans and shorts. And a person who would wear jorts? That is someone who will never truly find love.

I used to be harder on myself for being so judgmental. But then one day I heard Louise Hay or some other mediocre mind say, "It's easy to sit back and judge other people, but what we really need to do is have a harder look at ourselves," and I had a realization, a major epiphany really: it's not *easy* to sit back and judge people—I just happen to be really good at it! Sometimes we have to give ourselves a pat on the back for things we do well naturally and not just write them off because they come easily.

I came home from the stairs that day a little obsessed with getting my belly button pierced and determined to throw caution to the wind and just do it. And then I waited three or four years for my finances to be in better shape. Eventually I realized that I might never have forty dollars just lying around but that my stomach might not be flat forever, so I'd better make my move.

Luckily, I lived in Santa Monica, which is right near Venice, California, which is the piercing capital of the world next to, say, Africa.

"Andy, relax, I'm the one getting pierced," I said soothingly, and then knocked back my second shot of Jack Daniel's. It felt hot in my throat, and as it went down it slowly warmed my entire body from the inside. The effect was magical tranquility. I immediately felt sorry for people who do yoga—it's just so time-consuming and laborious. Show me a person who's into yoga and I'll show you a person who's never taken Xanax.

I'd brought along my friend Andy for moral support. Andy's not a drinker but during times of stress he turns to food, so while I was ordering my second shot of Jack he was desperately trying to procure a corned beef on rye. But this being a bar on the Venice boardwalk and not Jerry's Famous Deli, he was out of luck. Besides being a compulsive overeater, Andy was a compulsive worrier, but he was also really funny. We had been the best of friends since meeting each other doing stand-up seven years before. We had the one obligatory makeout session but before it could go any farther, Andy pulled away because he was getting treated for a nasty case of crabs. And, after cleaning all my bedding in scalding hot water and bleach "just in case," I told him we'd never be more than friends.

"Fine, just give me two orders of buffalo wings and a seltzer," Andy told the bartender. "And don't forget the blue cheese!" He was definitely nervous for me. "You don't have to do this. We can always blow it off and just walk the boardwalk. We could try to distract the guy who juggles chain saws instead."

"Getting your belly button pierced isn't something you just do on a whim," I said as I slammed my third shot of Jack. I assumed there would be a lot of pain involved. And any time there is going to be pain, you need to prepare by drinking.

The piercing dude at Tattoo U was underwhelmed by my enthusiasm when I burst through the doors demanding my belly ring. It possibly didn't help that I was accompanied by a Jewish lawyer. There was no one else in the place and yet I couldn't seem to get this guy's undivided attention, which was weird because I was holding up two crisp twenty-dollar bills as if I were trying to flag down a busy bartender. I kind of thought they'd be happy for the business. I mean, how often do people come in itching to plop down forty bucks? I had to figure that the overwhelming majority of people who have numerous tattoos and piercings don't also have jobs. Finally he came over.

"Have you thought about this? Are you sure this is something you want to do?"

"Yes. I've thought about it a lot. I have a belly that's just screaming out to be pierced. Look at it!" I raised my shirt to punctuate my point.

"I just need to know that you're sure. Piercing is serious business."

What kind of a newbie did this guy take me for

anyway? Did he not see that I had both ears pierced plus a double piercing on the left ear? Obviously I'd been in the piercing game a minute. Plus when I was twenty I'd had my nose pierced for six weeks. I had it done at an African-American hair salon in the Crenshaw district of Los Angeles, which was the only place that would do something so radical. I'd first seen the look on a British girl while drinking pints at the Cat and Fiddle, and although the trend had yet to reach the States, I knew I had to have it. Other than when I was taking a shirt on and off, washing my face, blowing my nose, grazing my nose with my finger, or being hit by a strong breeze, it didn't hurt at all. The *only* reason I bailed on it was that I couldn't get hired at any restaurants because they thought I was weird. But that was then.

Nowadays I was weird for *not* having a body piercing.

"I'm ready to do it," I told James, hoping my piercing authority was coming through.

I had to fill out a form releasing Tattoo U from any liability and making sure I didn't have any known medical conditions.

_____ I am at least 18 years old.
_____ I am not a hemophiliac (bleeder).

_____ I do not have a heart condition.

_____ I am not under the influence of drugs or alcohol.

_____ To my knowledge I don't have any physical, mental or medical impairment, condition, or disability which might affect my well being as a direct or indirect result of my decision to have any piercing-related work performed on me.

_____ I agree to follow all instructions concerning the care of my piercing while it is healing and afterward.

_____ I agree that any follow-up work needed, due to my own negligence, will be done at my own expense.

James and I both seemed to tacitly agree to ignore the fourth item but I got a little caught up on the fifth.

"Excuse me, James? I have a question."

"What's up?" James asked as he snapped on a pair of latex gloves.

"I have what my chiropractor refers to as a 'very low pain threshold.'"

James just looked at me.

"Well, I don't know if that's officially a medical condition that we should be concerned about."

"No. It's not a medical condition at all." This James sounded very sure, but I wasn't aware that piercers had medical degrees.

"I just need to have my lawyer look this over," I said, handing the form over to Andy, who looked like he might lose consciousness at any moment.

"Don't get any buffalo wing sauce on it, asshole." Andy was turning out to be fairly useless. I figured the least he could do was try to figure out if I had any lawsuit leeway if things turned ugly, but he was too busy snacking on the wings he'd taken to-go.

Finally it was time to get my piercing. I lay down on a padded table like you would find in any doctor's office and James pinched the skin above my belly button. I couldn't help but wince.

"Owwwwww!" This wasn't boding well for things to come, and to make matters worse, James was already looking very annoyed. I knew I'd have to make an effort to be more stoic since the last thing I needed was an irritable dude with a three-inch needle in his hand.

"Listen, hon. Maybe this isn't for you." I was not happy to be treated like a second-class citizen just because I wasn't sporting sleeves.

"No. No. No. I'm into it. Let's do it." The next thing I knew I felt a white-hot excruciating pain in my gut. The worst part is, it wasn't over quickly. James was leaning into it as if he were trying to pierce a bowling ball and not the delicate skin around my belly button.

Finally it mercifully stopped and I foolishly thought I'd survived.

"Now let's put the jewelry through," James said as if he were offering a paraffin dip with my manicure. I choked back screams as he jammed the metal hoop through the raw hole he'd just created. I honestly would rather have been eaten by a bear.

"Do you ever do this procedure under general anesthesia?" I asked. I mean, it was too late for me but perhaps I could help the next client avoid going through the same trauma.

After getting about four pages of aftercare instructions, I got the hell out of there to begin my new life. Sure, it had hurt like hell, but I felt triumphant. Now I knew what women who've given birth naturally must feel like. I mean, I really got it. I used to make fun of those people in the past because it seemed like a dubious honor to forgo drugs and really feel the experience. But now it was like, *yeah*. I was part of the sisterhood. I vowed right then and there to start spelling "woman" with a "y." My life as I knew it had changed. The sky was the limit now. I could join a beach volleyball team or become a belly dancer at a hip Moroccan restaurant or . . . the point was, it was done and I was a new woman—*womyn*—a womyn who constantly felt like she had to pee, as it turns out.

Four days after my piercing ordeal, I was heading to the bathroom no less than forty times an hour even though nothing was coming out. Not only did I constantly feel an urgency in my bladder but there was an uncomfortable heat that had taken up residence on my lower abdomen. I called James.

"Are you cleaning the ring?" he asked after he finally got on the phone with me.

"Yes. I mean, not all the time because it really really hurts. Like a lot."

"That's part of the healing process," he said as if he had a piercing line three deep, which I knew wasn't true. It was far more likely he was flipping through a tattoo magazine called *The Daily Prick* or something.

"How long should this pain last?"

"Maybe six months." *What the hell?* There was no mention of any six months of excruciating pain or even discomfort on the release form that I held in my hand while I cradled the phone against my neck. I thought about what I'd been through. If I could go through this, I could go through anything! Six months of pain was just fine with me. *Six months is not that long,* I thought. I could withstand anything for six months. Hell, I'd dated a guy with halitosis for seven.

Two hours later I'd had enough and I lay on my

living room rug with a pair of yellow rubber dishwashing gloves on my hands trying to get the damn hoop to pop open and come off. Every time I moved it I felt pain straight through to my spine. I wasn't entirely sure I wouldn't accidentally paralyze myself. I couldn't even loosen it without sending myself into another spasm of agony. "Cocksucker!" I screamed at the top of my lungs. "Fuck fuck fuck fuck fuck fucking fuckity fucker!"

"No, I need *James*," I cried to the chick working the front desk of Tattoo U. I slammed my still yellow-rubber-gloved hand down on the counter for emphasis. "Please, he has to get this off. Do you have some sort of piercing jaws of life?"

James appeared from the back room like some sort of vision. I loved him in that moment. And I sobbed. It's like when you hurt yourself as a child and you start pulling yourself together and then your mom comes over and you can't help but cry all over again. I wondered if James and I would end up getting married. People who have been through traumatic events together often form a bond. Perhaps he'd get my name tattooed on his chest. We'd have children together. I wouldn't want them to get their ears pierced though.

No matter how strongly he felt that our infant daughter should get her ears pierced I was going to take a hard stance on this issue. I just didn't feel it was right.

"Stand against the wall," James said with almost no tenderness in his voice. I did as he asked and in one quick move he clicked the hoop and pulled it out. Relief flooded through me and I fought back an urge to make out with him on the spot.

"That's going to be forty dollars."

"Forty dollars?"

"It's on the release: 'I agree that any follow-up work needed, due to my own negligence, will be done at my own expense.'"

"That's ridiculous. It cost forty dollars to have it done." Suddenly I wasn't feeling James anymore. I should have seen this coming though. Financial disagreements can tear apart even the closest of couples. As I was getting ready to leave I saw a barely legal girl walking out in front of me with a brand-new lower-back tattoo. And that's when it hit me that the thing I needed, the thing that would change everything, was a tramp stamp. If only I had forty dollars.

Graceland

"I'll never get that German sex shop grandma out of my head," I said to my brother.

"Ugh. That yuppie S and M couple was no treat either," my brother said as he splayed our AAA driving map across his lap. Due to an accidental viewing of *Real Sex* on HBO, the two of us already had a head start on bonding when we pulled out of the driveway in Springfield to drive him and his stuff out to LA. Really uncomfortable moments have a way of bringing folks together.

I'd come back east for my mother and stepfather's twenty-fifth wedding anniversary, and at some point during the festivities my stepfather asked if I'd consider taking his place escorting my brother on the cross-country drive. It was news to me that my brother was ever planning to make the trip with my stepfather in the first place. How fun could it be to drive across the country with your *dad*? Not nearly as entertaining as driving with your sister, I imagined, but I *still* wasn't sure it was a good idea. Although I was definitely fond of my brother, Michael, I didn't know him all that well.

When I moved to Los Angeles at eighteen years old, Michael was only eleven, a little kid, a pipsqueak. What does a rebellious, angry quasiadult have in common with a sixth-grader? But every year or so, I'd fly back east for Thanksgiving and my brother and I would find ourselves hanging out. When the family headed to our aunt and uncle's house for the big feast, my brother and I hid out in their basement watching football or lingered by the dessert table, stuffing ourselves with rum balls and secretly making fun of our extended family, not to be mean, but because it felt good to be on the same team. My brother became my comfort zone during those visits, which were often fraught with familial angst for me. The trip would end, however, and we'd go back to our respective lives, never so much as chatting on the phone until we met again the next year. I could count the times we spoke between visits on one hand.

I worried that when I was gone I was slowly becoming a ghost: a "black sheep of the family" ghost who flew back to haunt everyone for major holidays. I didn't want to be that to my brother and much younger sister, but living three thousand miles away, it was difficult to control my legacy. I imagined I was used as ammunition against my brother and sister's screwups. I assumed my parents held me up as an example of what can happen if you buck authority, forge absentee notes for school, break curfew, and argue constantly with your parents—and that was just the behavior they knew about. The fact that most of my visits home ended in some sort of high drama probably didn't help my cause.

But now my brother had graduated from Syracuse, spent a year living in New York City, and decided he wanted to move to LA, and I was being asked to go with him.

To spend a week in a car together seemed like an awful lot of togetherness and forced closeness that could spell disaster for even established relationships. On the other hand, I had nothing pressing to get back to, like a job or a boyfriend or a *life*, which sort of left me wide open for a road trip. So screw it, why not?

The night before we embarked my brother and I decided that the thing we must absolutely do to get ready for a cross-country adventure was eat a pot cookie. We fancied ourselves a couple of Hunter S. Thompsons in *Fear and Loathing in Las Vegas* minus the firearms and hard-core psychedelic drugs, and with only the possibility of a quick stop in Laughlin, Nevada. So to prepare for the cookie adventure, we'd stocked up on ice cream, chips, and other cliché munchies, turned on HBO to watch *Mr. Show with Bob and David,* and sat ourselves down in the basement of our parents' house waiting for the cookie to kick in when my stepfather popped in with a friend of his to "hang out." This setup quickly turned thorny.

Suddenly we were high and self-conscious. We couldn't dive into our snacks because it would seem obvious what we'd been up to if we suddenly pulled out our stash of Cumberland Farms mint chip ice cream, salt and vinegar chips, a couple of boxes of coffee-flavored Nips, Red Vines, and the leftover chicken soft tacos from dinner. My stepfather was no stranger to pot—in fact, he often bragged that back when he was managing bars in NYC in the sixties, he was the go-to guy for weed. To someone who passed a doobie back and forth to Bob Dylan and whose twenty-year-old denim jacket still smelled vaguely of sinsemilla, we would be instantly busted.

And so we waited. And then eventually *Mr. Show* ended and on the same channel *Real Sex* started. And my stepdad and his buddy were still there. *And nobody moved.* My brother and I felt paralyzed, unable to even steal a glance at each other for fear of bursting out in uncomfortable laughter. Segment after brutal segment featuring people who had no business being naked on television bombarded us while we sat there unable to retreat. It became a sadistic game of chicken with no one willing to turn away or even change the channel, thus having to acknowledge that we couldn't handle the situation. Eventually the show ended but the damage was done.

"Graceland isn't really my thing," I said to my brother on the second day of our trip. I had his portable CD player, which was plugged into the lighter, resting precariously on my lap and was trying to maintain a delicate balance so it wouldn't skip. "But since we're going to be driving within three hundred miles of it, it does seem foolish not to check out the King's final resting place—if for no other reason than to say we did."

"Agreed," my brother said.

"And to hit the gift shop," I added.

"Remember when we were little and Mom and Dad had to stop at every historical landmark?" my brother asked from the driver's seat.

"That was the worst."

"I seem to recall you refusing to get out of the car for most of those pit stops—which, by the way, I respected."

"I'm sorry, but I just never had a hunger to visit the home of Bumble Bee brand tuna. I don't care if it was considered a cornerstone of the Northwest's resource-based economy. I just wanted to stay in the car with my shoes off, reading."

"I hear you. They were all pretty boring. It was difficult trying to act like I gave a shit about something described as 'the finest example of mountain architecture.'"

"I could give a shit about architecture in general," I said, barely containing my glee at our shared apathy.

"Yeah, but I just never had the guts to flat-out refuse. Maybe it didn't even occur to me as an option. Defiance was more your territory back then. I was more the silent rebel type. A Jewish James Dean."

It was clear that my brother and I had more in

common than just our mother's shared DNA. I'd always suspected it, but now, being together, it was fact.

"I don't know if buying the headphones for this guided tour was our best use of funds," I said as we headed through the King's racquetball court. We had arrived at Graceland and were already underwhelmed.

"Something tells me that Elvis didn't play a whole lot of racquetball. At least not fat Elvis." My brother was bent over a metal drinking fountain installed against the wall. It was handicapped accessible. "And what are the chances that Elvis used this drinking fountain?"

"I say we skip the Elvis car museum. I'm not really jonesing to see his driver's license, are you?"

"I have a feeling Jay Leno has better cars just in his driveway alone. Not that I want to go to the Jay Leno driveway museum. And I think I saw those Elvis licenses in the gift shop anyway."

Next we passed through the Jungle Room, where Candy Spelling probably picked up most of her decorating ideas. *Since when does covering half your crap in leopard print make a room worth a stop on the tour?* I wondered.

"What I want to see is the toilet where he died. Didn't he die on the can?"

"I think so. Eating a sandwich, right? Or was that Mama Cass?"

"I can't be sure," Michael answered.

"You should know that. You're the one who went to college," I said. "I'm the loser who wasted time waiting tables all these years."

"I don't see you that way at all. I think you're brave."

"Thanks, Putty." I call my brother Putty because when he was really small—like a toddler—his little arms made me think of Silly Putty stretched out into human limbs. It wasn't a nickname that caught on with any other family members, it was just what I called him, and it stuck between us all these years.

Although it was late September, it was also Memphis, and it was hot as hell as my brother drove us away from Graceland and headed west as fast as possible. We wanted to get to Laughlin, Nevada, the next best thing to Las Vegas. Well, the next best thing to Reno, which was the next best thing to Vegas, but Laughlin was sort of on our way. We wanted to hang out at craps tables and drink Cuba libres with senior citizens in matching polyester pantsuits while screaming, "Come on, eleven!" We longed to stay in a tacky room, raid the minibar, order bacon cheeseburgers from room service, wear the hotel bathrobe around, and steal pens off of the housekeeping cart. This sounded like fun to us. It had been decided that when we got to LA my brother would stay with me for a while until he found a place. Just a week before this day I couldn't have imagined my brother staying with me for any amount of time and now rolling out the futon seemed like just the thing—an opportunity for me to lead the way.

Suddenly, without warning, red lights flashed behind us and a siren blared. A cop had pulled onto the interstate from his hiding place on the side of the road. Moments later my brother was handing over his license and registration, waiting to get his first speeding ticket in the state of Arkansas.

The cop handed it back through the driver's-side window. "This ain't an official driver's license, *Mr. Presley*. And it's not funny."

But it was funny. It was possibly the funniest thing ever.

Hometown Buffet

I'm seated in a booth with my father at Hometown Buffet, attempting to make myself disappear into the ripped vinyl seat while he verbally tap-dances for our waiter. "Pat, listen to this. I got another one for you: My dog had worms so I brought him to the vet. The vet said I should chop up little bits of garlic—you know, it's good for worms—and give it to him, so I did. Now his bark is worse than his bite." Stan's eyes twinkle and shine waiting for Pat's response. Pat laughs politely. It's not that he doesn't think it's funny, it's just that my father's told him this one before.

"That's a good one, Stanley." Pat, an older man, dressed in his Hometown Buffet polyester vest, just wants to bus the empty water glasses and continue on his way to another table, but to my father, an audience on the move is still an audience.

"You know, Pat, at the hamburger joint down the street they have a fruit salad that's reversible. If you don't like it, you can turn it over, and it's just lettuce." Pat chuckles.

This sticky booth at the buffet is a far cry from the main room at Caesars that my father filled during the late sixties. But attention is a drug, and my father is getting his fix. The only side effect is that it's impossible to have a conversation about anything that has taken place post-1975.

"I like that one. That's real good," Pat says, giving our table a cursory wipe with his towel, grabbing his bus tub, and moving on.

"How about some dessert?" Stan says to me, wanting to prolong our time together. "They have a dynamite bread pudding here. It doesn't have raisins. I can't stand raisins."

"I can't stand them either. I've never met a single dessert that I thought could be improved with raisins."

"See? We're exactly alike, Stef. That's why I like you. You're like hanging out with me." He takes a bottle of prescription pills out of the black satchel he carries with him everywhere and pops a couple. He does it pretty much every hour and I've given up telling him he takes too much. "I have headaches, Stef. This is the only stuff that works" is what he says when I nag him. He puts the pills away. "So, how about some of that bread pudding?"

"Bread pudding's not really my thing but I'll have a frozen yogurt. Come on." We get up and head over to the dessert bar to serve ourselves.

I stand behind him eyeing the display of soggy-looking puddings. I don't like the way he smells. He smells old. I feel mean just thinking that, and I resent him for making me feel mean. But it's the truth. He doesn't take care of himself and being with him reminds me of that—it drives home the reality that there is no one in his life to make sure that he showers, cleans up his apartment, or even goes outside to get fresh air. And I feel like he must be so lonely, and his loneliness, real or imagined, feels like a weight on me—an old familiar anchor that constantly threatens to pull me under. I really need to leave, to go home to my apartment, to my non-needy boyfriend. I want out of the whirlpool of emotion these visits bring up.

I pay the check with a credit card and Pat brings back the receipt for me to sign.

"Hey, Pat, what's that old shriveled-up thing on

Grandma?" Stan asks. Pat pauses, politely listening. "Grandpa!"

"All right, Stanley, I'll see you real soon."

"Stef, this is so great. You know what we should do?" I'm dropping him off in front of his apartment. I'm not going to go in, so I'm sitting waiting for him to step out of the car.

"What's that?"

"We should write a script together. It would be perfect. We could definitely sell a script together. A father/daughter team. Plus, it would be a great way to spend more time together, really get to know each other again."

"Stan, I can't do that. I have so much going on right now. I write full-time as it is. I thought you were working on your autobiography anyway."

"I am. I am. I have a lot on my mind right now. I have so many bills. It gets a little depressing, you know?"

"I do. I know. I have to go though, okay?"

"When am I going to see you again, Stef?"

"We'll go to lunch again in two weeks, okay?"

"Two weeks? What about next week? Hey, do you

want to take in a movie this weekend?" This is what always happens. It's never enough. And so I'm sinking again and I feel like if I don't leave right now I'm going to disappear.

"I can't. I have to go. We'll talk soon." He gets out of the car but leans his head back in.

"Listen, I'm doing a show on Sunday night at the Ice House. It's going to be my triumphant return! I really want you to come. Can you make it? Bring your boyfriend, what's his name?"

"Jon."

"Great! We'll make a night out of it. How about it?"

The whole way home I feel guilty. *This* is why I hadn't talked to the man in six years—*this* feeling. I'd managed to separate myself from *this* for six whole years until the night a few months back when I'd heard his voice on my answering machine and got sucked right back in.

"Stef? Are you there? I really . . . need your help. Are you there?" I recognized the slow cadence of a man with a lot of codeine in his system. But there was also something else, and the something else made me pick up the phone.

"Hello?" It was like no time had gone by, but *a lot* of time had gone by. A lot had changed. By distancing myself from him, I'd begun to get my shit together. If I was the type of person to say things like "I'd begun to blossom," I might say that. I had a boyfriend whom I didn't try to break up with every five seconds, a writing job, money in the bank. The bastard probably sensed it.

"Stan. It's Stefanie. What's going on?"

"Heya, Stef! You're there. I didn't know who else to call."

"What's going on? How are you?" I asked, bracing myself.

"You know, things aren't so good. I'm not really doing so well financially."

"I'm sorry to hear that." And I truly was sorry to hear it. But I couldn't allow myself to get caught up in it again. Ever since I'd moved to California fifteen years before and looked my father up, this had become our dynamic. I'd give as much as I was capable, his requests would steadily expand, and eventually I'd feel drained and angry, stop all communication, and then somehow get pulled back in. This time, I hadn't talked to him in six years. I was stronger now, I was happier; so I guess he sensed he'd have to up the ante.

"Stef, I hate to ask you but I need some money. If I don't get some money, I feel like I might do something."

"What do you mean *do something*?" He certainly had my attention now.

"I don't know, Stef. But I can't live like this. I can't go on." I always hated how he used my name repeatedly in conversation. It was like a car salesman: "Listen, Stefanie, what's it going to take to get you into a brand-new Skylark today? I know we can come up with a payment plan to make you happy, Stefanie." It felt like my father repeated the same shtick but personalized it for each audience.

"How much are we talking about?" I asked wearily. *What's it going to take to make this go away?*

"I knew I could count on you. I feel like if I don't get some money, I might end it."

"How much money?" Years before—with the help of a therapist—I'd made a decision not to give him money. But he'd never threatened suicide before. I had to hand it to him; this maneuver was a game changer.

"Just enough to get me back on my feet a little. I've been so down I haven't been able to teach, but if I could get out from under some of these bills, maybe I'd get a

little energy back. I'm an excellent teacher, you know."
I did know that.

"How much?"

"Maybe a thousand? I really hate to ask, Stef. I
didn't want to call my own daughter for money but
no one will help me out. My sister refuses to give me
a dime."

"Well, actually, I sorta remember from the last
time we spoke that after Harriet gave you a car you
called her a selfish pig." I hated myself for even saying
anything argumentative but I had a touch of Tourette's
when it came to my father. "Look, I don't have a thousand. Maybe I could help you out with a few hundred.
But I want to know where it's going. Do you need your
rent paid?"

"Yeah, I appreciate anything you can do. Beggars
can't be choosers, right? I'm just so depressed, Stef. You're
a good daughter." His voice sounded flat, defeated.

I try to suss out the severity of the situation, but I
was out of my depth. So after I hung up the phone I
called a hospital suicide hotline and talked to a counselor about the things my father had said.

"Any time someone makes a threat, we have to take
it very seriously," the counselor told me. "I'd like to
send a welfare check to his apartment."

"What does that mean?"

"The police would go by his apartment and check on him. How do you think he'd react to that?"

"It's highly likely he won't respond well. He doesn't care for cops." My father liked to think of himself as antigovernment, although I believe he was less antigovernment than antitaxes and anti–bill paying. He'd never paid child support to my mother or any of his ex-wives. At the time he and my mother split, he was headlining in Las Vegas for sixty thousand dollars a week. Lacking child support or any alimony, we ended up on government assistance within eighteen months. This was definitely unfinished business between us.

For a while I'd made the mistake of trying to make him answer for it, explain his actions, but he couldn't. I really had been trying to let it go and understand that it wasn't about me, it never was about me, but when he asked me for money, I still felt a sting.

"Listen," the counselor was saying, "this is a lot for you to take on. Let me send out a welfare check just so we can all be sure everything's okay." That sounded good. Peace of mind was always good.

My boyfriend Jon and I were getting ready to go out to a Christmas party later that night when I got the call from the counselor at the hospital. "The police are at your father's door knocking but they're getting no response. They want to call the fire department. I thought you'd want to know." Jesus. I had no idea what to think, so Jon and I got in the car, and rather than go to our friend's in Silver Lake to drink champagne and eat spinach-artichoke dip, we detoured to my father's Woodland Hills apartment. This wasn't how I wanted my boyfriend to meet my father but Jon wouldn't let me go alone, and I was grateful to him for it. When we pulled up to the apartment complex, there were emergency vehicles already there. A ladder truck and two police cars lined the front curb, so we had to park around the corner.

I had no idea what we would find at Stan's apartment. I hadn't even been there in so many years yet I found it easily without even pausing to check the directory. We took the elevator to the second floor, made a left, and headed down the hallway to number 206 as if I'd been there yesterday.

There were two policemen stationed at the door to his apartment, which was ajar. And just as we approached two firemen walked out.

"It's okay, ma'am, it's okay. There's no one inside.

He's not home. It's okay," one of the firemen said. "You can go in and see if you want." I hadn't even known I was crying until that moment. The firemen had broken into his apartment to investigate and found nothing but a lot of disarray.

"*This* is your father's apartment?" Jon asked.

"Yes," I said. Jon and I walked in tentatively; I felt I was intruding. Clothes were strewn everywhere; moldy towels were thrown on the floor; dishes covered every surface. There was a half-empty prescription bottle of codeine on his coffee table that was as big as a King Cobra malt liquor can. Who would prescribe that much medication? There were enough pills in that bottle to cure all the headaches in Canada. At first glance the place looked like it'd been robbed, but he'd always been this way, living in chaos. Plus, what intruder would make a huge mess but leave the drugs? No, this wasn't new, maybe just stepped up a notch. But seeing the mess through my boyfriend's eyes made it seem worse.

There was an empty glass cage that I knew was used to house a pet boa constrictor. I had a grisly thought that perhaps his snake had gotten hungry, escaped his glass enclosure, slithered into the living room, and eaten his cat. But then I saw a tail peeking out from under his sofa and when I bent down two eyes glowed at me curiously. So there was life.

Despite everything, and regardless of all my therapist's coaching, my so-called "healthy boundaries" quickly eroded when faced with this sad reminder of how he was living. I'd have to hire someone to clean this place. Just thinking that gave me a starting point; it calmed me. I checked out the bathroom, eyeing it like an amateur social worker doing an assessment. He was going to need some rails in the shower and maybe a few on the wall near the toilet. The last I'd seen him he was already frail beyond his years. I seriously doubted his health had miraculously been on an upswing.

Where the hell was he anyway?

The firefighters and police left, leaving Jon and me to sit down on the stained hallway carpeting to wait outside the door of the apartment for my missing dad. As we sat there holding hands, my heart rate sped up every time I heard the heavy groan of the elevator getting louder as it approached, only relaxing when the car creaked past en route to a higher floor. More than an hour went by before the elevator eventually stopped at our level and deposited Stanley onto his floor. He moved slowly down the hall toward us, looking downright dapper in a white shirt, his trademark newsboy cap, and a nice leather jacket. I didn't have a nice leather jacket.

"Heya, Stef!" he said brightly, as if finding me parked in his hallway crying was a pleasant surprise but not entirely unexpected.

"Where have you been?" I demanded, suddenly enraged to find him in such good spirits.

"I went to the movies with my friend Dave," Stan said.

"You went to the movies with your friend Dave," I repeated, incredulous. "You simply went to the movies?" I could not believe this shit. "Do you have any idea how worried we've been?" I asked, suddenly aware that since he hadn't been greeted by sirens, cops, and fully equipped paramedics walking around, he probably didn't have the full display of how successful his tactic had been, hence how frantically worried I'd become. "The police were here. I thought something happened to you. You said that you might hurt yourself. You said you were depressed."

"I'm sorry, Stef. My friend Dave called and offered to take me to the movies to cheer me up. I had no idea. But I'm tickled that you came. I'm thrilled to see you." It's as though I was returning to the scene of a crime over and over again. Don't they say that the definition of insanity is doing the same thing over and over but expecting different results? If that's the definition, then my relationship with my father was clinically insane.

"This is my boyfriend Jon, by the way." Jon had just been standing there not quite knowing what to do but trying to be supportive. He understood that this was a highly charged situation, and he didn't want to accidentally trip any wires. And really, what *is* the etiquette for meeting your girlfriend's father for the first time directly following a suicide scare? No one's really established that protocol yet.

That week I had his apartment professionally cleaned, flea-bombed, and disinfected. The Mexican couple I hired wanted triple their normal fee to make the place livable. Luckily the boa constrictor was long gone because I figured that would have definitely been a housekeeper deal-breaker. I paid his gas and electric bill, his long-distance phone bill; the things he hadn't dealt with were endless. I found a pile of bills from credit cards he'd applied for, gotten with a thousand-dollar limit, and then just never paid. There had to be ten or more. It crossed my mind that while he still had the acuity to fleece multinational banks, it seemed beyond him to run a vacuum across his floor.

I made a plan in my head that I would see him once every two weeks. Lunch. That would be *plenty;* I'd done more than enough to be able to live with myself. Lunch every other week would have to be enough.

Home Run

I've found employment on a lot of crappy shows during my television writing tenure: I've worked on *America's Funniest Home Videos*–style shows where I had to write Bob Saget–esque jokes over clips of fat people falling off roofs, grooms fainting during their nuptials, and dogs doing any sort of "they think they're people!" shit, not to mention figure out which wacky sound effect worked best over a video montage of toddlers swinging various sporting equipment into Dad's crotch. I've argued with a senior producer over whether or not a video clip of a raccoon in a swimming pool was best classified as "moonlighting as a professional pool cleaner" or just "out pool hopping." For the record the head producer wanted "moonlighting as a professional pool cleaner" but I felt that it wasn't right; I mean, if the raccoon was working as a professional, where were his little pool-cleaning supplies? Shouldn't there have been a long stick with a net at the end, or at the very least a floating chlorinator? So I'm not proud of all my jobs, but I've been able to live with most of my choices.

Even after a stint writing questions for *Strip Poker,* a show where women who couldn't answer general-knowledge questions were "punished" by having to strip down to a bra and panties, I was able to put my head on my pillow and sleep like a baby at night. Hey, my feeling was those girls had great bodies, which they probably paid good money for, and they were practically begging for any excuse to show them off. The only thing standing between them and an eager display of their plastic surgeon's handiwork were the network censors, so I didn't waste a minute feeling gloomy. In all these years, I've really questioned my morality only once, on a show called *Home Run,* so I think that's a pretty good record.

I might not have ever taken the job at *Home Run,* but I'd recently been fired from a new version of *The Three Stooges* after only three weeks and I was still a little in shock and looking for a way to redeem myself. It was a horrid job, one that entailed my having to watch old Three Stooges movies all day every day. The

Stooges shorts contained all the things that I don't like in movies: they were made before 1970, they were in black and white, they had no female leads, and worst of all, they featured physical comedy. This new incarnation of *The Three Stooges* was aimed at men who had sensed a void in their comic pantheon since Gallagher had limped into semiretirement. The only good thing about the job was that they kept two kinds of beef jerky on hand. I would have quit but I'd spent the first two weeks of the job learning an intricate file storage system for every frame of each Three Stooges movie, and I felt terrible leaving them to have to retrain someone else from scratch.

But that limited sense of obligation didn't stop me from complaining bitterly every chance I got. Although complaining has always been something I excelled at, I do know that it doesn't always help me get along with other people, except other people who also like to bitch and complain a lot. I like that kind of people.

I was fired in a private meeting in a conference room across from our offices so that none of my co-workers would be made to feel uncomfortable. It was the kind of firing that catches you completely by surprise, like back acne or a micropenis. When I strolled into the conference room, I couldn't help but think maybe the company was throwing me a little catered lunch to make up for the fact that I'd been working well below my pay rate. Instead, as I struggled to finish my cheek full of teriyaki jerky, I saw waiting for me my boss, her husband, and an HR rep. From my vast experience getting fired from waitressing jobs, I know the sight of HR means I might want to lawyer up.

The reason I was given for being let go was that I "poisoned the well." Apparently, someone had over-heard me the day before telling one of my friends on the phone that "this job sucks ass." That someone was the boss's husband, who sat right behind me. I calmly tried to explain to them that loathing my job with a passion and doing a bang-up job were not mutually exclusive, but no one wanted to hear it. Another writer had been sent to pack up my desk, and I was handed a cardboard box containing a spiral notebook with a few screenplay ideas in it (at least if anyone stole my ideas, I knew who to sue), a half-empty water bottle, and a sixty-day AA chip that had been left in my desk by the person who sat there before me.

"This isn't mine," I said, trying to hand it back.

"Mmmhmm. Why don't you just keep it?" my ex-boss said, which made me feel even worse. This was the first and only time I'd ever been fired since I started working in TV. So, although I was slightly relieved to be out of the situation, the fact that it had not been my decision stung my pride and left me determined never to let it happen again. I'd simply have to have a better attitude. As fate would have it, I was offered another job within the week. In the moment I thought it was a godsend. In hindsight, my slight depression, wounded self-esteem, and extra five pounds of sodium bloat may have left me vulnerable to making bad decisions.

"Okay, here's the idea: It's a half-hour dating show where two male contestants are set up with women for dates; they each pick a woman, go on a date, and whichever one gets the farthest with his woman wins. Of course, if one contestant goes all the way with his date, that's the home run!" Hence the brilliant name: *Home Run*. "The network guys pitched it to me and they want a not-for-air pilot. We need to shoot it in six weeks."

I was sitting in the office of Don, my potential employer. Don reminded me a little bit of Superman. He was a mild-mannered, nice Jewish guy from New York, but once he went into his office he turned into a hungry producer in charge of a fairly new but fast-rising reality TV production company. And he kept a big bottle of Sauza tequila in his desk, a quality I admired in a boss. Don wasn't in a position to say no to the network. And really, I wasn't in a position to say no to Don. "So before I agree, let me get this straight: The point is to sleep with your date? And the name of the show is not *Senior Prom*?"

"Ha, yes, exactly. It's a game show. We can give away refrigerators, cruises to Ensenada, all that. But the best part is the title: *Home Run,* right?" With his elbow on the desk, he rested his chin between his thumb and index finger and looked at me intently, waiting for my response, which could make or break this opportunity. I saw a few major problems. On the other hand this would give me a chance to redeem myself from my last job. I could show I'm a team player. A positive person!

"I love it," I said. "I'm in." And then I threw in, "Maybe we can find a way for it not to be absolutely essential for the contestants to have sex in order to win."

"Absolutely. I'm open. I leave that to you creative types."

A group of us sat in a small conference room for our initial production meeting. Next to me was the other writer/producer, Scott. Across the table sat our petite, blond field producer, Leanne, and a young geeky production assistant. After wrapping up a long, animated cell phone call that we witnessed through his office window, Don made a beeline for the conference room. "So, I just got off a conference call with the network guys, and there definitely needs to be sex. At least one of the couples has to hit the home run, at least for our pilot." From the second Don clicked his phone shut he was in type-A producer mode. This sex ruling was very bad news. I'd been holding out hope that once the job actually started, the original concept would shift considerably, maybe to a show about toddler modeling or giant tumors—you know, something tasteful.

"Well, we can't really control that. I mean, people either have sex or they don't. We can't exactly force them," I said. It seemed sort of obvious to me, a detail that would've been addressed before we actually started producing this show. In no way did I think we'd really move forward with the original horrific idea.

"That's the concept they bought. That's the show we need to deliver. Now, who wants a margarita?" Don's assistant walked in with a tray of margarita glasses. "What's wrong, Stefanie?"

All through this I'd been trying to force my face into a neutral expression, as if working on a show where I was less a producer than a pimp was just part of the business and not anything I found objectionable in the least. The problem with my face was (and still is) that it doesn't do neutral well—even when I'm perfectly happy. Unless I'm smiling, inevitably someone will ask me what's wrong. So when something actually is wrong or when I'm irritated, I look like I just got my first whiff of an angry skunk. It takes extreme facial control to look neutral—I usually have to overshoot for thrilled just to get in the neutral ballpark. "I'm just having a bit of trouble seeing how this is going to work is all." *Stay neutral, stay neutral,* I told myself.

"It'll work. You'll make it work."

"Well, except for one nagging detail: How do you give a guy a prize for getting a woman to have sex with him without possibly inciting date rape?" *Damn, that was so not neutral.* And apparently I was alone in this worry because Don stared at me like I'd just suggested the Holocaust never happened.

"Stop. No one's going to be raping anybody here," Don said. "No raping. I don't want that. Rape does not equal ratings."

"Try telling that to the producers of *20/20*," Scott

said. I was already pissing Don off and I'd been there only an hour. I was going to have to seriously step up my attitude upgrade.

"We need to inspire them," Scott said, throwing pencils at the ceiling Letterman-style. This was about as far from Letterman as any of us were going to get. "Inspire them," in dating-show speak, meant ply them with alcohol. Basically in any dating show, you need to provide booze. Well, booze and hot tubs. "We need to come up with some great date spots where our couples can get into the spirit of the thing."

"And take them there by limo," Leanne chimed in. Correction: booze, hot tubs, and limos.

"Why not just slip them ecstasy?" I said, finding this whole conversation more suited for a frat party.

"Is that legal?" Leanne asked.

"*No.* But somehow I don't think that giving a prize for getting someone to have sex falls inside legality either," I said.

"Shades of gray. Shades of gray," Scott said, making another hole in the ceiling. "That's the whole point of the show. The sex. That's what they want."

"I feel like we have to come up with something

else, some other things that the contestants can do to earn points."

Leanne the field producer sat by the window typing away like she was getting paid by the word. "Hey, Stephen King, what are you churning out over there?" I asked. I was puzzled since there was no show of any kind yet. Unless she was writing a novel, I couldn't understand what she could be so focused on.

"I'm making the crew schedule," she said as if that should've been more obvious than an albino in South Central. Scott and I turned to look at each other.

"What crew? There's no crew," Scott said, scratching his head with both hands in exasperation. I walked over to her desk to peek over her shoulder; this I had to see.

7:00 a.m. call time

8:00 a.m.–9

9:00 a.m.–10

10:00 a.m.–11

11:00 a.m.–noon

Noon–1

1:00 p.m–2 crew lunch

2:00 p.m.–3

3:00 p.m.–4

4:00 p.m.–5

5:00 p.m.–6

7:00 p.m. wrap

"Crew lunch? Why would you possibly have scheduled a crew lunch already?" I asked incredulously.

"They're going to be tired. They have to break for lunch; it's a mandatory union thing. There's really no way around it. We have to take care of our crew." She said all this like it was the most obvious thing in the world.

"Leanne, I'm sure it is, but we have *no crew*. We have no show yet. I think we should focus on figuring out what happens on the show before we schedule anyone's lunch."

"I'm a field producer. I schedule lunches," Leanne said. She was clearly going to be of no help.

A few days later, with the help of some books we'd picked up at Barnes & Noble about romantic hot spots (and a copy of *Best All-Time Tips for Quilters* that Leanne threw in the cart so the show would pay for it), we'd come up with a partial list of destinations for Leanne to scout. Whichever ones we could get for cheap would decide our itinerary. I was feeling no better about the job. I'd come up with an idea where we would give the couples "challenges" to do on the date to score points just to try to take the pressure off the end goal, but it hadn't gone over as well as I'd hoped.

"What kind of challenges? Sex challenges?" Don had asked when I brought it up in a meeting.

"Not exactly. You know, more like ridiculous challenges. Maybe making them do ten push-ups in the middle of the restaurant for points?"

"How is that sexy?" Don wanted to know. "How exactly does that lead to screwing?"

"Maybe they could do the push-ups naked?" Scott suggested.

"But not at a strip club," Leanne added, "it's impossible to get a permit." *How had writing for television led to having a serious discussion of naked push-ups?* I wondered.

"This whole thing is making me a little uncomfortable," I told Scott as we took a break and walked down Wilshire Boulevard to Starbucks for a latte. "I don't like the idea of trying to get people to have sex to win a contest. It feels very *The Accused* to me. It makes me feel slimy." Scott was wearing a Hawaiian shirt and mirrored sunglasses, so he possibly wasn't my best gauge of slimy.

"I doubt anyone's going to actually do it," Scott said. "I mean, unless we cast porn stars."

"Guys, this is Angela. She's here to audition to be on the show," our casting director, Lydia, said, leading Scott and me into the conference room a few days later. Angela was wearing a shiny black latex dress that couldn't have been tighter if it was her actual skin. The thing was cut down to her belly button and loosely laced up the front, barely containing her mountainous boobage—enormous even by LA standards. This girl definitely knew her way around an adult movie set.

"Problem solved," Scott said as we headed off to pencil Angela in for one of our first shoot days. The whole reception area of our office was chock-full of carbon copies of Angela, waiting, hoping to be on *Home Run,* the hot new show their agents had probably up-sold to them. I did have a momentary twinge. That had been me a few years ago. I knew what it was like to stand on the business end of a camera and now, thank God, I had a view from the other side. I liked this side a whole lot better and I was fairly determined to stay there, although at this point I felt it might require a lobotomy.

It was time for another sit-down with our boss; unfortunately it was Margarita Monday and he was a little tipsy. This was one of the perks of working in television: Margarita Monday, Tequila Tuesday, We Be Drunk Wednesday . . . after five o'clock, lots of jobs like to let things get loose. At my last waitressing job, if anyone had found out there was chardonnay in the lemonade I kept in a king-sized Styrofoam cup behind the napkins, I would have been asked to turn in my apron. In TV, breaking out the booze was just part of the creative process.

"I like this Carmen," Don said, holding up a head-shot from a pile of them strewn around the conference room table.

"Don, I'm pretty sure that used to be a dude," Scott said, looking more fascinated than disapproving.

"Whatever. She's hot," Don said.

"But check out the Adam's apple on her." And with that, the headshot got round-filed.

"I say we go with Angela," I said. "She really captures the spirit of what we're trying to accomplish here. And let's tell her to wear what she wore on the interview out on the date." Wow, I was starting to think like a *Home Run* producer, which was more than a little alarming, but the show needed to get made. I sort of felt like I was behind the scenes at a sausage factory; sure, sausage tastes yummy sitting on your plate with a scrambled egg and some hash browns, but once you know what they stick in those casings, your sausage-savoring days are over.

A week later, Scott and I sat in an edit bay watching footage of a drunk Angela modeling lingerie at the Hustler store on Sunset for her twenty-seven-year-old actor/musician date, who was the spitting image of Kato Kaelin. Leanne had secured the location in exchange for plenty of exterior shots of the Hustler sign plus B-roll of vibrating dildos and bondage harnesses. I guess the store was attempting to class up their image and thought exposure on a show like *Home Run* was the way to go. Luckily, Angela was clearly a loyal customer and knew her way around a crotchless-panty aisle. She made her way out of the dressing room in yet another next-to-nude getup, hopped up on Kato's lap, and started grinding on him. "Holy crap, did Angela just take a swig out of a flask?" We rewound the tape a minute and played it back in slo-mo. Sure enough, Angie was stealing nips between sticking her tongue in Kato's mouth.

"I think she might actually *do* this guy," I heard myself saying—gleefully, in fact. What was happening to me?

Once back in the limo, Scott and I could see by the lipstick cam we'd planted in the car that there was a full-on make-out session going on. These two were into each other; it was *on*. Thanks to us, that is. We'd done our job as producers—gotten them drunk and turned on—and now it was going to pay off. But then the limo stopped at Kato's condo, and after adjusting himself, he hopped out, gave his mic back, and teetered into his house alone. Nothing happened.

"Motherfucker," Scott said, slamming his Diet Coke on the edit bay desktop. "This dude couldn't close the deal. I really thought we were gonna pull this off." Didn't this really make more sense though? In real life people don't screw on a televised date, and they most certainly don't sleep with guys who sport such an obscene amount of Obsession for Men.

"Personally, I think it's for the best. Unless their

prize package included a lifetime supply of Valtrex, there's no way it would have been worth it."

I actually felt better about the whole thing despite the fact that we still had to tape the show in the studio in a couple of days. Maybe something would happen in the meantime: maybe old-timey radio shows would make an unexpected comeback, causing the network to scrap *Home Run* and focus their attention on finding a new host for *The Fireside Theatre*.

Somehow it had been left to me to brief Angela before she went out onstage during our pilot taping. Scott was assigned to Kato, who hadn't said much to any of us since the date. Leanne reminded us that she was a field producer and as such, her work was done here. She even had a formalized schedule to show it. Don made it clear to me that Angela needed to say that she'd scored a home run on her date, and in doing so, prove to the network that our show was perfectly producible. "You got it?" Don asked. To keep my face neutral this time I had to go beyond thrilled all the way to over the fucking moon.

"I'll do my best, but she didn't sleep with the guy."

"You're a producer; talk to her."

I wanted to be a team player, I really did. I loved working in television, and I never ever wanted to wait tables again, but this was a tough call.

Scott and I sat together in the control room watching Angela get grilled by the host, whose days as a big-shot network prime-time reality host were still to come. The network executives sat in director chairs, peering over our shoulders to get a closer look at Angela's breasts, which were so out of control they needed their own wrangler.

And then, the host got to the money question: "So did you or didn't you?" And it was completely quiet in the control room. All eyes were on a close-up shot of Angela.

"Oh, yeah . . . home run."

Out of the corner of my eye I noticed some quiet high fives around the room. Don fist-bumped the air, and Scott leaned over to me and said, "Dude! How'd you get her to say it?"

But I hadn't. That was the truth. I'd taken the high road. But that didn't mean I had to announce it to the room, right?

*   *   *

After the taping was through, and before the crew went out drinking, I went to the greenroom to find Angela. I had to find out what happened. When I poked my head in I found her packing up her wardrobe changes. "Angela," I said quietly, looking over my shoulder to make sure no one from the show was listening. "I'm so sorry if you felt you were pressured to say you had sex. I thought we talked about how you should just say what happened—tell the truth. I don't feel right about this." Actually, I had a whole mini confessional speech all worked out in my head for her, about my trying to be a better person, have a better attitude, but that I'd let my desire to please other people take over my judgment, which had all come together at the expense of her reputation. All of this was about to spill out to my makeshift father confessor in fishnets when she cut me off.

"But we did it."

"You don't have to say that to make me feel better. I saw the footage. All of it. He dropped you off and went home."

"Oh"—and here she giggled like a maniac—"I guess there was something you didn't see. We screwed in the dressing room at the Hustler store."

"Huh." This was a surprise. I thought I'd been in

control of this situation somehow. I thought this was all up to me. I was a typical self-important Hollywood producer and in the end, Angela was the one truly calling the shots. And unlike me, she seemed mighty comfortable in her role. But this was good. I'd gleaned some valuable information from this gig that would surely help me moving forward: never underestimate the inherent sluttiness of a wannabe reality star. Lesson learned.

"Well, good luck, Angela!" I said as I made my way out. I said it but I knew she wouldn't need it.

Hi, Angie

Hi, Angie,

I hope you don't mind if I call you Angie but I feel like I know you because a friend of a friend of my brother reads the *National Enquirer* and always catches me up on what's happening in your life. So first off, I know that you already have like a boatload of kids but that you just recently added twins to the mix. And I heard that you are finding twins to be very challenging. Actually the friend of a friend of my brother said that you are "totally going out of your mind." I think you should know that I too recently had twins. Not as recently as you and not in France. Although I did eat a lot of croissants while I was pregnant and my ass got huge. In fact, I don't really know what this *French Women Don't Get Fat* author was thinking, but she got her facts wrong. I mean, seriously, eating a croissant is like eating a stick of butter. This might explain why I haven't shed all of my pregnancy weight.

But on to the real reason for my letter: twins are a bitch. It's seriously underrated the toll it takes on your anxiety level, mental stability, physical appearance, and overall health in general. Anyone who tells you with a huge smile that you must feel "doubly blessed" deserves to be punched in the head (but have Brad do it, because you need to save your strength). When I had my first baby, she slept in a bassinet right next to the bed and, sure, I woke up eighty times a night, but it was okay because she was the only baby and I expected to lose some sleep. Scratch that; it wasn't okay, I was a hot mess, but it was livable. One night my husband (who looks slightly like Brad—I'm not gonna lie, he's a looker!) suggested that he sleep in the living room with the baby so that I could get a full night of sleep and I just about took his head off. I accused him of not loving me and just wanting to sleep alone. When the twins came—let's just say, completely different story. We took turns sleeping on the couch for months and I was thrilled every single time it wasn't my turn. Like I said, twins are a bitch and it's not your fault.

I have one nanny during the day, and I hear you have a few on hand so I'm assuming you have one at night. Hell, you probably have a nanny dedicated just to reapplying your lipstick. Doesn't matter. All the help in the world can't drown out the crying of two babies who refuse to sleep, eat, or play at the same time. Please don't believe the people who will tell you to "get them on a schedule," because that does not work on the planet reality. Personally, I'm not big on showering (wow, maybe I *would* fit in better in France), mostly because I have only about half the amount of photo shoots that you do, but since I've had twins I can count the showers I've had on one hand without using my thumb.

There's not a whole lot you can do right now to make things better. You could try the

Duggars' method and just have one of your older children, Maddox or Zahara or Dax or Ping Pong, watch the younger ones—but you'll still have to keep an eye on them. Don't take this plan to the bank though, because I've tried it, and my three-year-old still acts like her sisters don't exist. Plus, my daughter likes to dress up as a princess and whack people with her magic wand. Apparently babies don't like this game. At all.

I guess what I'm trying to say is, you don't have to be strong for any of us twins moms. We get it. We laugh in the face—right in the damn face—of people who have one baby. We think even moms of twins who don't have another child (or four in your case) are weak if they complain. We've earned the right to be complete psychos. So you go, girl, interrupted. And if you end up in the loony bin for a couple of days or months, I will be your first visitor—provided you don't mind a couple of crying babies in a double stroller and a whiny three-year-old coming along.

Listen, in a few months, this will all seem almost amusing and you can just send a turkey lasagna to Rebecca Romijn with your sympathies. Which reminds me, I wonder if J. Lo ever got the apple pie I sent. I never received a thank-you card. Rude! Anyway, best of luck and call me anytime! Well, any time before nine p.m.

Sincerely,
Stefanie Wilder-Taylor

Oct. 10, 2008

Hi again, Ang,

I swear I'm not stalking you. Seriously, it's just that after I wrote you that last letter responding to the whole twins situation, I kind of thought we were on the same page about how difficult it is. But then, I find out that you posed for a big fancy magazine breast-feeding your babies and looking all serene and Mother Earthy. Like breast-feeding twins was just the most natural thing in the whole entire world. I couldn't help but feel it was sort of a slap in the face. Admittedly, I haven't actually seen the pictures, so maybe you were wearing nipple shields and they got airbrushed out and maybe there was a Boppy involved, or frozen cabbage, or at the very least some damn soothing lanolin, but I doubt it. Well, kudos to you on your success, Angie. Fine, I'm probably a bit jealous.

I could tell you a whole long story about my failed yet drawn-out attempt to breast-feed my first daughter and how I smelled like fenugreek for at least a year, which is forty-eight weeks longer than I actually breast-fed, but you don't have time for that. Not with all that breast-feeding you're doing. But I did quickly want to share with you that I was all cool in my decision not to even try to breast-feed when I found out I was having twins. If one was hard, two would be hell, right? I mean, sure, I knew I'd have to get an unlisted number so that the La Leche League couldn't call and lecture me or picket outside my house, but I was okay with that. But then I found out much later on that my twins would be born prematurely and all my resolve flew out the window. Those preemies, they need the breast milk. I knew I'd have to give it and them my best.

You probably don't know this, but two preemie babies plus two milk-challenged boobs equals frantic pumping. Hang on, I have to go lay down for a minute just thinking about this. Okay, I'm back. Maybe you should just give me your number so I could call you; if anyone could breast-feed twins and talk on the phone at the same time it would be you . . . Anyhoo, the very day my twins were removed from my stomach, the nurses wheeled in this huge hospital-grade pump with tubing and funnels and a motor so big it could start a car. It looked like some sort of medieval torture device. The thing sat next to my bed about three days, untouched. I know I was on a lot of pain medication but I swear through the haze I heard it taunting me. But I couldn't let it intimidate me.

When I got home from the hospital with no babies, I immediately started pumping like it was my job—every day, all day—then I'd head to the hospital with my proceeds. Even on a good day I couldn't fill a Nyquil cup with what came out, and just to get that much I needed breast-feeding porn. I'd look at pictures of my babies or a friend's babies while I pumped. When pictures of my own babies stopped working I got desperate enough to go on preemie baby websites just to try to get my breasts stimulated enough to produce a little milk. Nothing helped, not pumping right in front of the babies (and the entire NICU), not having a big glass of dark beer, not fenugreek, not different-sized funnels, not lactation consultants, nothing. My friend Shannon even offered to give me some of her breast milk 'cause she was gushing like a fountain with her baby, but the NICU frowns on illicit street milk. Anyway, by the time I brought my babies home, I could maybe get a dropper full. It was useless. So I stopped. I cried a day or two, tried again, and then gave up for good—although the rental breast pump stayed in my living room mocking me and accruing a balance for an extra three months because I was too busy with the twins to return it. It was like the world's most expensive late library book.

I guess my point is that you are super lucky you're able to breast-feed those cute babies, but do you have to show off about it? Aren't you perfect enough as it is? I already feel guilty that I haven't adopted any kids in the last ten minutes; now I'm feeling bad about being a breast-feeding failure all over again. I think

I liked you better when you were struggling. Honestly, those bountiful breasts of yours look like they were made for milking. And no, I'm not embarrassed to say that I've checked out your rack. Come on, I'm not the only straight woman around who's thought about them from time to time. Okay, a lot . . . maybe I am stalking you . . . Anyway, if you ever want to grab a coffee, call me. On second thought, you can't have caffeine. Hmm . . . maybe I'm not so bad off after all.

> Keep in touch,
> Stefanie Wilder-Taylor

April 7, 2009

Angie,

Hi again, how are the kids, how's Brad, blah blah blah . . . ARE YOU HAVING *ANOTHER* BABY?? Oh my God. Are you insane, woman? I know you may find this hard to believe but I am truly not stalking you. I mean, stalking is such a harsh term, don't you think? It's just that it's hard not to notice you, being that every time I go to the grocery store (which is every day because I have a lot of kids—although "a lot" is relative because I actually have only half as many as you and Brad), I see your ridiculously glowing face and am forced to read some new rumor about you. The latest being that you're pregnant again. I can't believe that's true; I mean, my twins are older than your twins and I wake up every day thanking my OB for having the good sense to tie my tubes.

Maybe I shouldn't take everything you do so personally. I'm sure you don't mean to try to one-up me—or four-up me, as the case will be if you have another baby. But seriously, stop it. You're making me look bad. How am I supposed to whine on a constant basis to anyone who will listen to me about how sucky my life is with twins and a toddler when you are going around having babies as often as Joan Rivers goes in for a nip/tuck? This twins thing is really hard—like mind-numbingly hard. We talked about that, remember? I can barely leave the house every day by nine a.m. with one of my children (although that child, who shall remain nameless but is four years old and still very into Ariel, feels the need to spend *an hour and a half* picking out just the right tank top to wear to school when it's forty degrees outside in the sun), yet you manage to haul the entire brood back and forth to France and then off to somewhere like Bangladesh to run a food bank or film a political epic like you're just stepping out to grab the mail. Every time I see a picture of you, you've got a kid in each arm, two in Brad's knapsack, and a few more trailing behind. *And you want more.*

I'm still mourning the fact that I had to buy a minivan. When my husband drove me to the Honda dealer to pick up my new Odyssey, I think I knew exactly how a dog feels when it's being driven to the vet to have its testicles chopped off. Sure, my husband put some kick-ass flames on the sides to take some of the sting out of driving a total mommobile, but they're magnetic flames, because it's a lease. So not cool! Whatever antidepressant you're taking is the hardest-working drug in showbiz, because I would be crying in my bathtub with a bottle of Bombay gin right now if my husband even hinted at having more kids.

Why are you trying to make me look bad? You're not even back up to your pre-

pregnancy weight from the twins. I don't think you should be allowed to get knocked up again until you've at least packed on ten or fifteen pounds! Aren't there laws about this? Don't you ever just make a big old pot of Kraft mac and cheese, only to find that Pax refuses to take even one bite, so then you just go to take a little taste to see if there was a problem with it—like the powder didn't mix in well enough with the pasta, butter, and milk—and next thing you know you wake up next to an empty pan with a big old wooden spoon in your hand and a telltale bright orange mouth? Obviously not. Haven't you ever bought full-fat Ben & Jerry's ice cream "just for the kids," only to have Sahara or Ex-lax cry, "Mommy ate all the Cherry Garcia! Bad mommy. Bad mommy!" sending you into a shame spiral until the next time you buy a pint and devour it mindlessly while watching the latest rose ceremony on *The Bachelor*? Are you even human?

You don't have to prove that you're more than just a beautiful face. We get it. Sure, it was weird when you were doing irresponsible starletish things like marrying Billy Bob and talking about bringing knives into the bedroom, but it's not like you shaved your head and went to a mental hospital. You've never even done one single stint in rehab. So why all the effort to prove you're superwoman?

You win, Angelina. You had me at the whole breast-feeding twins thing. At this point you've got Jon and Kate shaking in their boots. I bet even the Duggars have you on their radar. Please, Ang, I'm begging you mom to mom, stop trying to make motherhood look so easy. Now if you'll excuse me, I have three tons of laundry to fold, a vomit-covered bath mat (don't ask) to clean, and a duvet to disinfect (has to do with the whole vomit situation). But I'm sure you have to go anyway. You probably have a red carpet to walk.

Please keep our talk in mind,
Stefanie Wilder-Taylor

Thank You,
That's My Time

S tan was raring to go the night Jon and I picked him up for his big show. Everyone loved Stan at the Ice House. "I'm a hit here, Stef. I've always been a hit here. I'm just glad you came to see your old dad do a show," he'd said before we stepped out of the car. I knew he was excited that I'd agreed to come; he was eager to show off for us, to make me proud. But I was extremely nervous for him, partially because I had no idea of what to expect. I'd avoided many of my father's past performances at the Ice House even during periods of steady but limited exposure.

Years earlier, just after I'd moved to Los Angeles and gotten back in contact with my father, I'd gone

with him to this same club and been accosted by one
of his comedy students. Kitty was a weird woman I'd
disliked on sight. She took me aside and wanted to
know why I wasn't "doing something" about my father.

"He has a serious pain pill habit and he's not in
good shape. I can't believe you've allowed it to get this
bad."

"I haven't 'allowed' anything. I have no control
over what he does." I was furious and defensive. This
chick was no picture of health herself, and I recalled
that at some point she'd gone through a nasty divorce
and spent a good deal of time on my father's sofa,
where I suspected she'd shared the fruits of Stan's doctor shopping. But now she was gunning for a fall guy,
and I was it.

"You need to talk to him," said Kitty, emphatically
pressing on. She didn't know, and likely wouldn't have
cared, that I'd attempted to speak to Stanley many
times about his drug problem, but with no success.
Like a classic addict, he had zero interest in hearing it
and would get downright livid if pushed on the matter.
I had a better chance of convincing him to undergo
gender reassignment surgery than to abandon his be-
loved pain meds. At the time, it would still be years
before recovery chic was in the offing, so there was no

Dr. Drew Pinsky to stare empathetically at me while stressing that I was neither responsible nor to blame for my father's habit, which predated my birth. So instead I stood there in the middle of the Ice House, sputtering denials at Kitty, crushed by the weight and ferocity of her accusation. At least fifteen years had passed since that incident, but I never knew when she was going to pop up in the crowd at one of Stanley's appearances so I'd steered clear.

I didn't want any trouble tonight. I needed this to go smoothly. I had Jon with me, and he'd never seen my father perform. He'd only heard me talk about Stanley and how much I respected his talent. Jon had seen the articles and bits and pieces of press I'd collected about Stan over the years. I wanted Jon to see what I saw, but more than that, I knew just how desperately Stan needed the crowd to love him and reassure him that what he had to offer was still wanted.

It wasn't a great sign that Stan seemed particularly scattered that evening. Jon and I had taken him to dinner at the Cheesecake Factory, where he planned to go over his set with us, something I'd been looking forward to. I wanted to hear the jokes first, remind him which were my favorites and what to let go of. But the restaurant was overcrowded with the Sunday early rush, which meant kids, which meant screaming, and the acoustics were so bad we were unable to have any conversation other than yelling, "Can we get some more bread?" at the waitress. I've been known to carb-load when I'm nervous.

Stanley was performing in the Ice House Annex, which was a smaller room than the main showroom, used mostly for showcases and comedy classes. It was also the room where Stanley had done most of his shows over the past few years. Tonight it was sparsely filled. Lots of chairs sat empty, and the audience was clustered in small groups spread around the room. I couldn't tell if he was disappointed or if this was par for the course.

Stan paced in the lounge area while Jon and I took our seats. I wasn't sure how Stan felt, but I felt completely unprepared and I needed to calm down, which for me meant a drink and some nachos. People may judge but microwaved Velveeta over corn chips has always had a medicinal effect for me. It didn't help matters that our cocktail waitress was in our face immediately, overzealously reminding us of the two-drink minimum. Having cocktailed in comedy clubs before, I was initially sympathetic, but this one was on a mission.

"What would you like for your drinks?" she asked, as if she were being timed for efficiency. Jon ordered a vodka rocks while I ordered white wine and a plate of the numbing nachos, but she wasn't satisfied. "What would you like for your second drink?"

"Well, we didn't get our first drink yet," I said, trying to sound reasonable, although I was feeling anything but. The comedian who was up just before Stanley had been riding the red light, which meant he was overdue to wrap it up. I glanced back and saw Stan walking—his slower and less deliberate form of pacing—back and forth across the rear of the show-room. My heart beat erratically. I needed my wine now, I realized.

"I have to bring both of your drinks at the same time. There's a two-drink minimum and this ensures that we sell both drinks." What was she talking about? Two drinks at the same time?

"Trust me, we'll order a second drink. Can you please just go grab our first ones?" I stammered, sound-ing less reasonable by the moment.

"It's our policy to bring both drinks or at least charge you for both up front."

"Fine, bring both drinks now," my boyfriend said. Smart man. And all at once, the waitress moved on to harass another table, the comedian onstage stepped off, and the MC appeared to introduce my father. I knew I couldn't control what happened when he went onstage; I couldn't control the audience's reaction. I couldn't control whether they had a good sense of humor or if they tended more toward "You might be a redneck if . . ." jokes. But I was hoping that there were people there just to see him. *He's going to be fine,* I told myself. *He's done this so many times, in so many places* . . . Stan was much funnier than I could've ever hoped to be, and yet . . . it had been such a long time since he'd been up in front of an audience, and his mind had been dulled by medication and age.

I sat in my chair with my boyfriend by my side as Stanley was introduced. "Ladies and gentlemen," said the MC, "we are lucky to have a legend in the house tonight. You may remember this man from all the shows: *The Ed Sullivan Show, The Dean Martin Comedy Hour,* and *The Tonight Show.* Please welcome the great Stanley Myron Handelman!"

Stan made his way down the path through the center of the audience and up the stairs to the stage; when he stepped up and turned to the audience his face softened with the confidence of forty-plus years of performance experience. But from the start, something was off: "I almost didn't make it here tonight. My house was robbed. A guy broke in and . . . and . . ." He'd set up the joke but couldn't remember where it was going, let alone recall the punch line. His brain wasn't doing him any favors tonight. There was uncomfortable silence while he went off on a tangent trying to joke with the crowd a bit, letting them know that he used to be on television. I wasn't quite sure if he knew he never reached a punch line to his first joke and it wasn't clear if the audience knew either. But if there was any doubt, it was eliminated when he started off another joke and got lost in the middle. At this point, I knew his act better than he did and was determined to assist.

"What about your uncle?" I said loudly enough for him to hear me from the stage, and for everyone else in the small venue to hear me too. "Didn't you just lose an uncle?" Thankfully the spark ignited and Stan's mind came to life a bit.

"I just lost a very close uncle of mine . . . My best uncle . . . We were mountain climbing. It was an awful, awful tragedy. We almost made it to the top too . . . we were like fifty feet away and he fell right over the side . . ." I sat frozen in my seat, my face flushed, because I realized he couldn't remember the rest. Trying to throw him a lifeline, I stage-whispered, "His last words, do you remember his last words?"

"I'll never forget his last words," Stanley announced. But he had forgotten. He seemed like he couldn't quite access the end of the bit he'd told a thousand times. I knew exactly how it finished: *My uncle said to me, "Stanley, you have a terrific sense of humor, you should really get someplace in show business," and he remembered when he was a little kid how he always wanted to play the harmonica . . . and then something about his mother . . . it was hard to make it out because he was all the way near the bottom.* It was the bit that never failed. But even from eight feet away, my being able to recall it was of no help. The unique voice Stanley had possessed, the ability that had gotten him what modest acclaim he had found in life, was gone. He fumbled, trying to divert attention to people in the audience, making small talk with the crowd.

It pained me to see the crowd—and himself—so clearly out of his control. The stage was the one place where my father had always been in the driver's seat, but now, suddenly no one was at the wheel. I was terrified for him but I couldn't save him. He was on his own.

Graciously, the audience, out of pity, sentimental-

ity, or just to help diffuse the tension, chuckled here
and there when Stanley ad-libbed while meandering
through his act. I couldn't help but feel lucky this
wasn't taking place in one of the New York clubs, because when New York crowds sense weakness they'll
eat you for brunch. But even with the generosity of the
crowd, this may have been the most uncomfortable
situation I can recall. I watched the stage intently while
Jon watched me. And I felt for my dad. I felt for him
onstage because a part of me was up there too.

Mercifully, Stan had reached the light, indicating
the end of his allotted time. I didn't know how much
time had gone by; it could have been ten minutes, it
could have been twenty, but it was time to end it. I
didn't like people feeling sorry for him; I didn't want
anyone to feel the way that I did.

Stan saw the light and he looked past it, taking
in the audience and his surroundings. I felt his eyes
search the crowd and settle on mine. But he wasn't
with me, not by a long shot. He was in performance
mode, buffered by a combination of adrenaline, pills,
and scattered laughter. In spite of the missteps, this
was a feeling he couldn't let go of. He pressed on,
starting a setup to a joke I'd heard many times before.
I could feel the tension spread through my body as I

hoped he could pull it off, but his timing felt jerky and erratic—like an engine that won't quite turn over: "I was walking near a park. There were some . . . this group of ruffians, these hoodlums, they were attacking a mailman." The audience listened politely, knowing this was probably the end. But as Stanley continued, he stumbled into a little groove: "These punks, they were grabbing all his mail, tearing it up and tossing it all around. I was horrified. All of a sudden, this old man walks over to me and he says, 'Look at those kids. God bless 'em. I wish I had their energy.'" A medium-sized laugh erupted from the audience and Stan, finally acknowledging the light, reluctantly said his thank-yous and good-nights.

"So? What'd ya think, Stef? How was it?" My father's eyes were lit up with post-performance rush. I deflected his question with a lame response that I've always hated when people use it on me coming offstage: "How do you feel!?" Along with "Well, *I* thought you were great," or "How do *you* think you did?" "How do you feel!?" is the all-time biggest cop-out in that situation. Of course, it's nothing more than sly code for "I'd rather drink straight out of the Comedy Store toilet than give you an honest account of what just happened up there."

Luckily, Stan didn't notice my pivot.

"Good. I feel really good. Nothing feels better than putting on a great show."

Jon shook my father's hand. "That was great, Stanley."

"Thanks, Jon. I still got it, don't I?" Jon looked at me and slung an arm around my shoulders.

"It's something I guess you never lose," Jon responded. And I wondered what he was thinking, but it didn't matter, because we were walking out the door to finally go home.

Drink, Drank, Drunk

I'm an alcoholic. It's an ugly word but I've come to accept that it's just a word, and if I can remain honest with myself, it does describe me fairly accurately. I haven't always had a drinking problem. I obviously didn't stagger out of the womb a little seven-pound, three-ounce Amy Winehouse. I don't know if I was born an alkie but I definitely think I had a propensity for addiction from the get-go. It's surprising since my parents are Jews—some of the least-likely folks to pass along addiction besides maybe to salty food. In my childhood I assuaged anxiety by binging on Halloween candy or going for thirds of macaroni and cheese. Certainly growing up in an environment where overindulging in food was the only accessible and effective way to turn down the noise in my brain may have helped postpone the inevitable, but I do believe the drinking habit was preordained.

The first time I ever got rip-roaring drunk I was fourteen years old. It was on Everclear grain alcohol punch served out of a high school classmate's bathtub. I don't remember much after the second shiny plastic cupful except that I puked all over my adorable Guess one-piece yellow romper and my best friend Tanya tripped down some stairs on the front porch and sprained her ankle. Everclear is about 80 percent alcohol, which is something like *1,000 proof,* and the liquor, in certain potencies, is illegal in several states. But in Spokane, Washington, when it came to drinking, we didn't mess around. I'd heard it said back then that my high school had one of the worst records of teen alcohol and drug abuse in the state. I'm not sure if that's true and I'm too drunk to Google it right now (kidding) but it sounds about right. Once I had my first foray into serious partying with the hard-core drinking crowd, I was pretty unstoppable.

The memories of those binge-drinking weekends are like looking through a shoebox with a tiny hole cut out of the end—the type of thing you would use to view an eclipse: there I am, sloppily making out with a boy I liked in the moment, and then, in the next glimpse, I'm swapping spit with a different guy an hour or so later. I can smell the beer and feel the hangovers, brutal hangovers where I threw up all day long, barely able to lift my head from the pillow.

Saturday mornings in Spokane I had Hebrew school, which my mother had decided was an absolute necessity of the Jewish culture. Many Saturdays I managed to beg off sick—stomach flu! Migraine! Cramps! But when my mother had had enough of my excuses and forced me to go, I usually spent the better part of the morning engaged in a fierce battle of wills between my brain and my nauseous stomach. The day of our Hebrew school confirmation, while the rest of my class received their honors, I puked my guts up in the temple bathroom. Mazel tov to me.

The first time I quit drinking I was fifteen.

I drank *a lot* with my best friend Tanya. It just seemed like the thing to do—the only thing to do. For a long time we drank every single weekend night without fail, not thinking that we drank more or less than anyone around us. We drank in crowds, on bluffs, in parks, huddled around kegs and chugging Miller Lite with everything we had. Everyone got drunk at these gatherings, so drunk. That was the point.

We called it "choir practice" and on Friday afternoons, word on where that night's choir practice would be held snaked rapidly through the student body like a gasoline fire. At Friday night's choir practice, Saturday would be drunkenly planned. Tanya and I went on like this week after week, until one day, seemingly out of nowhere, the idea occurred to us that our drinking habits seemed excessive. We wondered to each other why it was so difficult for us to do anything *besides* drink in all of our social downtime. And so, before it got too out of hand, we issued a challenge to ourselves to live our lives free of alcohol. We made big plans: We'd go to basketball games! Join the Junior Achievers! Go out to movies! The list was endless and we were on a mission; we could do this!

The first thing that became clear was that Spokane was an incredibly boring place to be sober. I believe we lasted about three weeks—give or take two weeks. I didn't know it then and I would've laughed in anyone's face who tried to tell me, but this was probably the first sign that alcohol played too big a role in my life, that I needed alcohol to feel normal, like I was on the inside looking out instead of the outside looking in. So I went back to my weekend boozing, picked up right where I left off. It seemed like the much simpler thing to do.

For many years, food played the bigger role in my quest to stave off strong emotions and anxiety. Food was my vacation spot, the place I went to when I needed to tune out, disappear from uncomfortable feelings, or simply feel entertained (which is most of the time). It made sense; food, after all, was my first friend—food and I "got" each other. Eventually, like a lot of women, I entered a full-on battle with an eating disorder, going to meetings, reading self-help books, sitting in therapy. But as crappy as having an eating disorder is, as shameful and hopeless as it sometimes felt, it almost made me feel normal, like wearing a pair of trendy Calvin Klein jeans or being a child of divorced parents. I certainly wasn't in the minority. I wasn't alone. I had a problem with food, but not with drinking, because *that* would be unacceptable.

Through my twenties, I did get drunk, pass out, black out, drive drunk, vomit, cry, and wake up hungover and full of remorse. But not *every day*! Plus, *everyone* in their twenties and early thirties gets drunk by accident sometimes. It wasn't so unusual to wake up in the morning after a night of particularly heavy drinking and nervously peer through my bedroom blinds, hoping against hope my beat-up yellow Mazda would be tucked securely in its tandem space, because if it wasn't I wouldn't have any idea where to begin looking.

Every once in a while I questioned my drinking but always managed to convince myself I wasn't that bad. *Alcoholics were not like me,* I told myself. Alcoholics drank in the morning—like my high school math teacher who sipped vodka and orange juice out of a coffee mug all day thinking no one knew, figuring we didn't notice his hands tremble as he held the chalk, attempting to help us find the value of X. Alcoholics got the shakes. Alcoholics certainly didn't maintain jobs and pay their bills semiregularly. Alcoholics drank to get drunk. *I* didn't do any of that. When I got drunk, it was almost always an accident. I'd had too much wine the night before on an empty stomach or was subjected to too many free drinks. I was in a celebratory mood or very very sad. There was a reason. I certainly didn't have a *problem.*

The second time I quit drinking my oldest daughter was two and a half.

When Elby was born, my drinking ratcheted up to an almost daily habit. To deal with the stress of new motherhood, I'd turned to evening drinking, allowing myself to sink into a bottle of wine when circumstances didn't allow me any other way I could see to relax. I found myself so looking forward to my wine that I began a bit earlier and then even earlier at night. I loved to cook because my pasta sauces were about eighty proof, and before I was done cooking I had a nice buzz going too—a splash for the sauce, a splash in my glass, little more for the sauce, a lot more for me. This evening ritual was a solace for me and eventually, like a stream of water rolling down a rock, my behavior wore a groove. Drinking wine felt like home. It was my comfort, the only way I knew to feel good. And as a mother, it was the only thing I felt I had just for me. I told myself that I wasn't hurting anyone so what was the big deal? I never ever got drunk around my child. I was available and loving. I just liked to drink at night. But there was a nagging voice arguing with me. That voice sounded a lot like my liver.

"I feel fat and bloated," my liver would say.

I'd counter as if I were dealing with a whiny teenager. "You're not fat."

"I've been working way too hard lately. You keep promising me you'll give me some time off and then you renege."

"Renege, huh? That's a pretty fancy word for a liver."

"Okay, now you're making fun of me."

"No, no I'm not. I'm just tired too. I need a way to

take the edge off. Just one more night and then I'll give you a rest. I promise."

"You say that every night," my liver would say, pouting. "You need to stop."

And it was true. I'd started bargaining with myself: *Okay, okay, I will give you a night off. I will only drink on weekends.* But then I'd think, *That's nuts! What person who rarely leaves the house can only drink on weekends? I'm stuck at home every evening. I deserve to at least have wine to entertain me. I think a much more reasonable idea would be* not *drinking on weekends but drinking every* other *night.* Of course by Friday night I would see the folly of my plan: *I can't not drink on a Friday night! Who doesn't drink on Friday night? It's a night for celebration! They call it TGIF! I didn't invent the term! Plus, Friday isn't technically the weekend, it's more the end of a workweek, so not drinking on Friday isn't even logical, therefore as a thinking, logical person, it makes a lot more sense to drink on Friday, and while we're making sense, Saturday doesn't seem like a good night to abstain either.* Sunday would have to do. Only after a few Sundays of not drinking, I'd forget why I was even trying.

One Halloween night before Elby turned two, I got drunk taking her trick-or-treating. My sister-in-law, Racquel, took me aside a week later and told me she was a little concerned about my drinking. No one had *ever* in my life expressed concern over the way I drank. She was so very gentle in her approach, unlike my bossy liver. "I'm just worried . . . Why are you checking out? . . . Are you depressed?" I acknowledged that yes, I was probably drinking too much wine at night and, yes, I'd definitely take a look at it. And so I tried once again to cut down and a few months later when I found that once again, cutting down was just too hard, I quit. And about six weeks after that I found out I was pregnant with twins.

Many women will say that for some unknown reason it's pretty easy not to drink when you're pregnant. Could be the hormones, could be just the fact that you know you can't, but I found it to be the opposite of a struggle to abstain from alcohol for those nine months which, naturally, made me question why I'd been questioning whether I had a drinking problem. Obviously not.

I was under an extreme amount of stress with those darn twins. Between the colic, the failure to thrive in my little one, the NICU stay, the hospital bed rest, and an ill-timed visit from my in-laws, it's a wonder I wasn't sent for a stay in Shady Acres. I slipped back into my old drinking habits with the same palpable relief of getting back into my pre-pregnancy jeans. My nondrinking period had just been a minor hiccup, necessary maybe but not realistic. This life I had now absolutely required alcohol, and to think it didn't was almost laughable, so I didn't give it much thought for a while. I drank because it made me feel better at night. I drank because it was finally "my time." I drank because I simply had to take the edge off from all the screaming I'd just endured. It's not like I could just head off to the gym or go get a massage or a pedicure—at this point, painting my own nails would've been a luxury.

For a while, the wine did help take the edge off, but at some point—and it's really hard to explain—it just kind of turned on me and it was no longer fun. It was something I had to do every night. I didn't even like the feeling anymore. I just drank because I couldn't ever think of a reason not to. But I didn't have a "problem." If I tried to quit drinking I'd have a problem, so I just gave in to it, rolled around in it like it was a deep, soft feather bed. "I'm just someone who needs to drink every night," I told myself. "I'm a drinker—that's who I am. And it's not hurting anyone." But those quills were poking through.

In only a few short years I'd gone from drinking to unwind to drinking to self-medicate, to finally just drinking—not needing a reason to and rarely finding a reason not to.

One morning I woke up on the couch hungover and I found myself at a crossroads: I could promise myself not to drink like that again, knowing full well I'd break that promise. I could admit to myself that, although my drinking hadn't gotten me in trouble yet, it suddenly seemed clear that it was only a matter of time. As a wife and mother to three young children, I had an awful lot to lose, and if I didn't find a new coping mechanism, I would surely lose it. Maybe not today, and maybe not next week, but why sit around with my infinite glass of pinot grigio and wait for bad shit to happen? Right then and there I made the scary but ultimately freeing decision to get help.

Stopping the actual drinking was a beginning but honestly assessing my past drinking patterns and realizing that mayhaps being too hungover to take my SATs at sixteen wasn't completely typical behavior—not even in the ballpark—and *possibly* not everyone attempts to drink their way through colic (although if any reason was a good one, it was that!); and for most people, crying on first dates is the exception, not the rule . . . I'm not going to lie, there have been times when not drinking is still harder than anything I've done; I've been a pinball game of emotions, zipping from ecstatically happy to homicidal in an afternoon, not knowing how to simply be.

It seems to me that because I worked so hard to avoid the simple lows, I inadvertently couldn't experience the simple highs. Now I get them all. And it's mostly good. The other night I was playing a rousing game of Candy Land with Elby when I realized something: I was always the sort of mom who would be down for a game with the kids but I'd do it knowing that there was an end point and that end point included an adult beverage. All of a sudden I got it; Candy Land is the point.

So, yes, I'm an alcoholic and I don't like the word any more now than I did when I first had to admit that the word applied to me and not just the red-nosed woman I see panhandling in front of El Pollo Loco, or random department store Santas, or Andy Dick. There are various degrees to alcoholism, various stages, enormous variations in the degree to which we devastate ourselves and others, but the super-simple thing we all have in common is that we shouldn't be drinking. Hey, novel, right? But as a recovering alcoholic, a lot more descriptions of me are accurate now as well: decent wife, dependable friend, good mom—the kind of mom who's always down for a game of Candy Land. And that . . . is pretty darned sweet.

Dear Dave

August 18, 2009

Dear Mr. Hasselhoff,

Actually, may I call you David? I'm assuming I can because you seem super down-to-earth and not held up on formalities—in fact, since we're being casual, maybe I could just call you Hoff, since that's what I call you to my friends. Okay, so it's settled; Hoff it is!

Here's the thing, Hoff: I wanted to touch base with you because it's come to my attention that I have a problem with alcohol, and due to a certain YouTube video featuring you sans shirt eating a burger on the bathroom floor, I know you have struggled with the hooch in the past as well. According to more recent speculation, you may be trying to kick the "cravings." Maybe we could hang out and not drink together? Scrabble? Badminton? Poker? Listen to seventies ballads and talk about our feelings? Any of these activities pique your interest? I just think that we could have a good time and possibly be a positive influence in each other's lives.

I know to the casual observer it might not seem like we have much in common besides our crazy love of booze, but I prefer to think of our similarities rather than our differences. For instance, you're huge in Germany; I'm . . . pretty well-known at my Encino Trader Joe's—let's just say I'm on a first-name basis with the lady who mans the sampling station! In fact, when I bring the twins there, we pretty much cause a commotion of cuteness. Let me put it this way: I've taken thirds on the chicken enchiladas and she didn't blink an eye. Oh, there's more: You starred in *Baywatch* for many years and I once Rollerbladed right past the spot where you were filming the show! Seriously, right past. Okay, I don't know *for a fact* if you were filming the show at that exact time because there weren't any "production vehicles" or "cameras" per se, but I did see a lifeguard stand and someone in a red bathing suit who looked a lot like Pam (Anderson) (well, the blond part). You know what, whatever, I'm not going on record here. Let's move past that.

According to Wikipedia, where I get all my important information, you once did a movie called *Legacy,* which also starred a Filipina actress named Chin Chin Gutierrez. Um, just so happens that I eat in a restaurant right here in Los Angeles called Chin Chin *all the time.* Although it's not Filipino food, it's Chinese, but they make the most fabulous chicken salad and steamed dumplings. If you order the dumplings, ask for the garlic-soy dipping sauce though, because otherwise they'll just bring you regular soy sauce, which is not nearly as tasty. I bet you already know that because I think you might live in LA— just another thing we have in common! This is getting downright crazy! We're absolutely meant to be sober buddies.

Oh, you know how you used to drive that talking black Trans Am in your show *Knight Rider*? Well, guess who else drove a black car?

Yes sirree, bob. I drove a black Volvo S60 for a number of years until I had twins and was forced kicking and screaming into a silver Honda Odyssey. My husband still gets to drive the Volvo though, which I'll admit causes some resentment. I mean, why should the sweet ride (a practically new 2001 with only 67,000 miles on it) be considered "his" car now? Are the kids "my" kids? No. This is probably something that deserves further investigation at another time. Maybe when we get together you can give me your thoughts.

So, I know you have a lot going on, *as do I,* Hoff. But I feel we need to put our sobriety first, and if that means leaving some things on the back burner so we can get together and talk then that's what we need to do. What's happening with *America's Got Talent*? Are you still hosting that? If so, maybe I can come down to the "set" and we can kibbitz. Also, I have a cousin who is a wonderful balloon-animal artist and if it wouldn't be a bother, maybe you could get him through the first "civilian" rounds of auditions and straight to the show? Take my word for it that this guy is good! I've seen him make a snake that would knock your socks off! Just give me a time and I'll be there wearing my "Don't Hassle the Hoff" T-shirt as long as you promise not to wear leather pants.

Stay off the sauce,

Stefanie Wilder-Taylor

Shooting Up

In 2008, I had three kids, a husband, and a lively writing career, which was the culmination of years of stand-up and television writing jobs. But still, after all these years of building myself up on the inside, getting therapy, reading motivational books—okay, *watching* motivational Lifetime movies—I was still not immune to the pressures of living in Los Angeles. I tried to be; I went weeks without getting my brows waxed; I rarely wore makeup 'cause I figured, why bother? I'm a writer! I have earned the right to stay in my pajamas all day and temper deadline anxiety with Red Vines. If I miss a day or two of moisturizing, who's counting? I haven't been to a commercial audition in over ten years, I have no agent fretting over whether or not my J. Lo booty is going out of vogue and maybe I should do Pilates because they heard it can really lengthen your glutes. I'm free of feeling the need to conform to the whims of society's ever-changing standards of beauty. Although, I don't know if I ever actually thought about it in those terms or if I was simply too lazy to do anything about my retro bush (oh yeah, I rocked the pizza slice for months after I had kids) and mustache. But I did pride myself on my lack of self-consciousness.

But one day I caught sight of myself in a photo snapped at a four-year-old's birthday party and my smug attitude took a sudden and consciousness-altering nosedive. I couldn't believe what had happened to me. One day I was young and cute and the next it was like the elements had declared jihad against my face. I immediately phoned my best friend Diana. "*Fuck*. I look forty—and not the good kind of forty, not Salma Hayek forty. I look *regular* forty. I might need some kind of emergency intervention."

"Honey, it might be time for us to get Botox," Diana said gingerly, taking on a big-sister tone. A few years prior to this I wouldn't have even considered putting toxins in my face, because a few years ago I had been laughing my ass off at how ridiculous Meg Ryan looked with her crazy lips the size of banana slugs and how Nicole Kidman's face packs more plastic than my wallet. And then I had a kid. And, oh my God, in one year I aged ten. And then I turned forty and got pregnant with twins and suddenly, there I was looking forty-two and feeling fifty.

"Botox. That sounds expensive. And there are needles involved—not a fan. And don't you have to do it all the time? Isn't it addictive?"

"Well, sure. If you're crazy. And rich. And an actress. We are none of those things, therefore I think we can be trusted to tox responsibly." She did have a point there. But I was still nervous. "Look, I'm going to see my dermatologist next week for a mole count; why don't you come with me and we'll ask questions?" Pathetically that actually sounded fun. But when you have three kids, your fun threshold is significantly lowered.

When she swung by my house to take me with her to her Beverly Hills skin doctor, it occurred to me that this is something only women do together. You'd never hear a guy say, "Dude, I'm going to get my toupee clips rotated, wanna ride along?" But Diana and I had it like that. We did everything else together, so why not this? I figured I'd let Diana do her thing and then I'd slip in a few questions for the doctor—as if the questions just occurred to me that instant and not like I was trying to work in a free consultation.

Of course once I was in the vicinity of medical personnel, I was off and running. "Can I ask a question?" I said to the assistant nurse. And then I dove right in. "So, I'm going to the gym, I'm eating healthy, if you consider Healthy Choice ice cream bars to be healthy, which I do—hello! The word 'healthy' is right in the name!—I'm getting enough sleep, and by 'enough' I mean a few hours bookended by children crying and getting into bed with me every night. But basically I'm doing my part and yet, my age is starting to show. I was thinking about the possibility of a little Botox."

"You know what would be great for you?" the assistant nurse asked.

"Um, what?" I said, hoping whatever it was, it would be available in a cream.

"We have this new mini face-lift. It's nonsurgical and it requires only a few days of social downtime." Was she serious? Did I really look like someone who could use a face-lift? This was very disconcerting.

"I'm only forty-two. I think that's a bit young for any procedure requiring 'social downtime,'" I snapped back.

"I know you'd love the results. My mom did it and she looks ten years younger." Could she make me feel any worse? "It's only two thousand dollars. We're running a special." Apparently she could. "Of course you could always go with Botox and some filler if you're trying to save money. But it may not get rid of those furrows completely." And here she poked the top of my nose with her index finger to illustrate, in case I wasn't aware that my face was a freak show. *Damn. I may not be able to get rid of my furrows completely?* This was bad news since I hadn't even known that what I considered a cute little scrunch my nose made when I smiled—like a little bunny—were furrows. Such a nasty word. Furrows sounded like the tunnels in the ground made by rodents overrunning the backyard. Wait, I might've been thinking of burrows, but in any case, whatever they were, they were in my forehead.

"I want to look ten years younger but at this point I'll settle for a little rested," I said to Diana on our way home from mole patrol, "because I certainly don't have two grand lying around for a face-lift."

"That was pretty ridiculous," Diana said. "You don't need a face-lift. Maybe just a little tox and a laser."

"A laser? Why do I need that?"

"Those liver spots aren't going to lighten themselves." This was worse than I thought.

"I don't know. Maybe I could just try getting more sleep."

"Stefanie, let's be honest, you're the mother of three little kids; the chances of you having Botox far exceed the chances of you getting a full night's rest."

It was a few days later at our daughters' school Halloween carnival that I scoped out a potential Botox referral. "We can't just ask Cheryl who does her face," Diana said when I pointed out a friend of hers with flawless skin.

"Sure we can! It's a compliment," I argued back. "If she hasn't had Botox she'll be thrilled to know that she looks that good naturally. And if she has had Botox, she'll feel flattered that it's working!"

Two weeks later Diana and I sat in a chiropractic/laser office ready to get a face full of poison. We were both a little nervous. "So what if I'm not an actress and so what if I will never again look twenty-seven; is it wrong to want to get carded at nightclubs and have the Mexican guys working on the house next door stare at me and say dirty things about me to each other in Spanish?" I said.

"Then again, who even uses a term like 'nightclub'

besides someone in their forties? So we're probably not fooling anyone anyway," Diana said.

"I deserve to erase some lines. I may have three kids and spend an inordinate amount of time in sweatpants watching *Caillou,* but I would like to look in the mirror and not see a big old frown line across my forehead. Is it too much to want to not look permanently scowly? That chick at your doctor's office said I have furrows!" I'd truly done a one-eighty since I'd seen myself in that birthday party photo, but there was no turning back now.

Before we could deliberate any longer, a statuesque woman of indecipherable age came to fetch us from the waiting room. "Hel-*lo,* dahlings! Come in and let me make you beautiful." And with that, we were safely placed into the proficient hands of Zara. Zara was like Joan Rivers minus the accent, one-liners, and furs. But like Joan, she had a face that had clearly never met a procedure she didn't like. And the woman was a genius with a needle. Zara's hands worked so fast they were a blur of ice rollers and syringes full of Botox, covering every inch of my face above the cheekbones.

"Dahling, you won't see anything for at least a week. But, trust me, you will look amazing. You will not belieeeeve the difference. You will *love* it." She over-enunciated the word "love" for maximum dramatic effect, which Diana and I would repeat over and over for weeks to come. "Do you want to try capers on your bagel, Stef?" Diana would ask innocently. "You will *love* it!"

The truth was, two weeks later, my face frozen with botulism, I did indeed love it. I couldn't get over how great I looked. There was only one slight problem: I couldn't wink.

"Look, Di, when I try to wink I look like a stroke victim," I complained to her after the Botox had fully set in.

"True, but who winks anymore? That's one facial expression that's been completely unnecessary since 1977. Good riddance! Plus, you look fantastic." And it was true.

My forehead had the appearance of an ice-skating rink just after the Zamboni works its magic. I was receiving compliments right and left. "You look so rested; your babies must finally be sleeping," an acquaintance of mine who didn't know my secret said to me one day.

"Thanks, yes, this twins thing is finally getting easier," I lied.

For the next four months, I enjoyed putting on

makeup again because my skin was so smooth. I felt younger, more energetic; there was a spring in my step. *This shit was a miracle.* But it was also expensive, and even after only doing it once, I knew very soon I was going to need to score more. My mind started working the angles on how I'd get more. It was going to cost money to keep up my new habit, but I didn't care.

Six months after the first time I shot up, I did it again.

And then five months later I was back for another boost.

It was so much money. Did it make me a bad person? A vain person? I was just not ready to go back to the way things used to be. I wasn't proud of myself for feeling this way. I wouldn't want my daughters worrying excessively about how they look on the outside, nor would I want them injecting botulism into their face to ward off age, but I certainly wouldn't judge.

I couldn't help but wonder if anyone had ever knocked over a dermatological office to steal a few units of Juvederm. I could sort of understand. Once you've had a taste of looking younger the desire to keep it up can make you desperate.

I know the healthier attitude is to accept growing

older gracefully. My husband calls my wrinkles "laugh lines" and insists that they are a natural part of me and give me character, but that's just because he knows how much a syringe full of Botox costs—he sees it on the Visa bill every ~~six~~ ~~five~~ four months. But hey, at least I'm not getting a face-lift. Yet.

Acknowledgments

This is the hardest part because I have a lot of people to thank. Let's start with the book folk: Patrick Price, my talented editor, I'm so lucky to have you on my side, on the other end of the phone, and at the receiving end of my manuscripts. Jen Bergstrom, Tricia Boczkowski, Jennifer Robinson, and everyone else at Gallery, thank you, thank you, thank you. I have an amazing team and I'm so grateful. Thank you for continuing to believe in me and continuing to give me money to write books. It's beyond words.

Andy Barzvi—getter of jokes, giver of encouragement. Thank you for being my agent.

The JPP Jane, Kim, Kristin, Megyn, Emmy, and Alex—thank you for being in it with me. And Marielise—I'm crazy grateful for your guidance.

Diana Horn—my BFF, personal photog, sounding board, and Tox buddy, how is it that we never get sick of each other?

Liz Gonzalez—yes, it's done. Can you believe it? Once again, thank you for watching my children while I wrote, slept, and ate Trader Joe's French toast. You are irreplaceable and so missed.

My brother, Michael Wilder, sister-in-law, Racquel, and neph, Beck—thanks for being my family and a whole lot of other stuff.

My gorgeous gals Elby, Sadie, and Matilda—I love you guys so much it's ridiculous.

Jon, you know all the things I said to you in the acknowledgments in the first three books about how you're my rock and I couldn't have done any of it without you and how you're so good-looking and how I couldn't ask for a better husband? Well, take all of that and *double it*!